At Issue

Is China's
Economic Growth a
Threat to America?

Other Books in the At Issue Series:

At Issue

| Is China's
| Economic Growth a
| Threat to America?

Ronald D. Lankford, Jr., Book Editor

GREENHAVEN PRESS
A part of Gale, Cengage Learning

Detroit • New York • San Francisco • New Haven, Conn • Waterville, Maine • London

Elizabeth Des Chenes, *Director, Content Strategy*
Cynthia Sanner, *Publisher*
Douglas Dentino, *Manager, New Product*

For more information, contact:
Greenhaven Press
27500 Drake Rd.
Farmington Hills, MI 48331-3535
Or you can visit our Internet site at gale.cengage.com

For product information and technology assistance, contact us at

Gale Customer Support, 1-800-877-4253
For permission to use material from this text or product, submit all requests online at
www.cengage.com/permissions

Further permissions questions can be emailed to permissionrequest@cengage.com

Articles in Greenhaven Press anthologies are often edited for length to meet page requirements. In addition, original titles of these works are changed to clearly present the main thesis and to explicitly indicate the author's opinion. Every effort is made to ensure that Greenhaven Press accurately reflects the original intent of the authors. Every effort has been made to trace the owners of copyrighted material.

Cover image copyright © Images.com/Corbis.

LIBRARY OF CONGRESS CATALOGING-IN-PUBLICATION DATA

Is China's economic growth a threat to America? / Ronald D. Lankford, Jr., book editor.
    p. cm. -- (At issue)
    Includes bibliographical references and index.
    ISBN 978-0-7377-6185-6 (hardcover) -- ISBN 978-0-7377-6186-3 (pbk.)
    1. China--Foreign economic relations--United States. 2. United States--Foreign economic relations--China. 3. China--Economic conditions--2000- 4. United States--Economic conditions--21st century. I. Lankford, Ronald D., Jr., 1962- editor of compilation.
    HF1456.5.C6I8 2013
    337.51073--dc23

                                                                2013001151

Printed in the United States of America
1 2 3 4 5 6 7 17 16 15 14 13

Contents

Introduction

As the Chinese economy became larger and more influential at the beginning of the 2000s, analysts and politicians repeatedly asked: will Chinese economic growth harm the growth of the US economy? Although US manufacturing seemed to be losing jobs to off-shoring (American companies contracting with China), exports of agricultural goods for US farmers expanded. The results, then, seemed both good and bad.

The positive results, however, did not prevent trade disputes between China and the United States. In international trade, Chinese companies expanded into former US strongholds; in the United States, domestic companies shipped more manufacturing jobs to China. Further, competition grew between the two countries for world resources such as oil and steel. In these ways, the growth of the Chinese economy has led to increased tensions in both economic and diplomatic relationships with the United States.

One area of trade, however, was rarely mentioned in the debate or the statistics—military budgets and arms sales. While US military spending and arms sales have outpaced every competitor, China increasingly showed a willingness to compete on the world's stage in both areas. These changes have greatly complicated the relationship between the US and China, none more so than in the economic sphere.

On one level, China's entry into the world arms market offered the same problem as China entering any other world market. Relying on cheaper labor and government aid, Chinese companies had a competitive (if not technological) edge on the world market, potentially underselling US products.

This potential for competitiveness became clearer following the near collapse of the world economy at the end of 2007 and the beginning of 2008. While world arms sales decreased overall, the United States and China both expanded their sales of weapons and military goods to supplement other losses in trade and revenue during the recession. "China's growing influence in the market is fuelled by its desire for natural resources," noted Ben McPartland in *France 24*, "and its willingness in a global recession to offer military aid or cheaper deals in exchange for natural resources rather than cash."[1] In 2011, US arms sales tripled, mostly by selling to the Middle East, while the Chinese were increasing sales in Africa and other countries. "China's arms exports have surged over the past decade," wrote Colum Lynch in the *Washington Post*, "flooding sub-Saharan Africa with a new source of cheap assault rifles and ammunition."[2] Richard Weitz concurs: "The People's Republic of China (PRC) looks set to become an increasingly prominent global arms seller thanks to its improving defense industry."[3]

While it was clear that the Chinese had increased arms sales, Chinese military exports and imports were difficult to track because of the lack of public statistics. Unlike the United States or Great Britain, China has kept much of this data private. "There are few official statistics on the Chinese arms trade," noted Amnesty International, "but the Stockholm International Peace Research Institute estimates that [China] accounts for around 3 per cent of the global trade in conventional arms."[4]

If China continues to increase domestic military spending, many observers believe that it is important for the United States to "keep up." While Chinese military spending does not come close to equaling that in the United States (the United States surpasses all other countries in military spending), it has grown quickly over the last ten years. In 2002, the Chinese military budget was $20 billion; in 2012, it was $120 billion. "The United States still spends four times as much on its military," noted Keith Richburg in the *Washington Post*. "But by some accounts, China is on course to surpass the United States in total military spending by 2035."[5]

Even the United States's biggest advantage—technology—may be erased over time. Chinese military purchases, for instance, were sometimes seen as investments: once an advanced weapon was purchased, it could be used as a starting point for understanding new technology. The new technology, in turn, would allow the Chinese to replicate and sell more advanced weapons on the world market. Also, China continued to buy technology illegally on the black market, including purchases from US defense contractors.

An arms race between the United States and China offers the same potential for an economic crunch that occurred between the United States and Russia during the Cold War. As more and more of the national budget is dedicated to arms expenses, funds that directly and indirectly aid economic development (education, research and development, and infrastructure) are potentially limited.

Current competition between China and the United States for arms sales may seem minor as China and the United States are often selling different types of arms to different markets. However, the US government is actively searching for ways to broaden its arms sales. The easiest way to accomplish this would be to liberalize rules pertaining to which countries would be allowed to purchase weapons. "Defense firms, which could reap huge benefits if exports policies were streamlined and restrictions loosened," wrote J. Michael Cole, "patiently await the decisions by Congress and the State Department on the matter."[6]

The economic relationship between the United States and China will likely become increasingly complex in the coming years. Markets in both countries have become dependent on one another, and the potential for growth seems promising for many industries in the United States and China. Military budgets and arms sales, however, add a volatile element to the economic relationship between the two nations. The contributors to *At Issue: Is China's Economic Growth a Threat to America?* examine from many angles the complexities of this relationship.

Notes

1. Ben McPartland, "China's Presence Grows in Murky World of Arms Trading," *France 24*, August 23, 2012. http://www.france24.com/en/20120307-china-arms-trade-africa-sudan-usa-uk-business-military.
2. Colum Lynch, "Chinese Arms Exports Flooding Sub-Saharan Africa," *Washington Post*, August 25, 2012. http://www.washingtonpost.com/world/national-security/chinas-arms-exports-flooding-sub-saharan-africa/2012/08/25/16267b68-e7f1-11e1-936a-b801f1abab19_story.html.
3. Richard Weitz, "Controlling Chinese Arms Sales," *China US Focus*, October 18, 2011. http://www.chinausfocus.com/peace-security/controlling-chinese-arms-sales.
4. "The 'Big Six' Arms Exporters," *Amnesty International*, June 11, 2012. http://www.amnesty.org/en/news/big-six-arms-exporters-2012-06-11.
5. Keith Richburg, "China's Increasing Military Spending Unnerves Neighbors," *Washington Post*, October 23, 2012. http://www.washingtonpost.com/world/asia_pacific/chinas-increasing-military-spending-unnerves-neighbors/2012/10/23/4b66a7ae-1d29-11e2-ba31-3083ca97c314_story.html.
6. J. Michael Cole, "U.S. Seeks Foreign Arm Sales," *Flashpoints*, September 10, 2012. http://thediplomat.com/flashpoints-blog/2012/09/10/facing-defense-cuts-u-s-seeks-foreign-arm-sales.

1

China's Cooling Economy Puts Obama Export Goal at Risk

Kathy Chu

Kathy Chu is an Asia reporter for the Wall Street Journal.

In 2010, the Barack Obama administration set a goal of doubling exports to China in over five years. In fact, during the first two years that followed, exports exceeded expectations. The balance of imports and exports with China, however, remained uneven and the United States continually ran an export deficit with China. As the Chinese economy began to slow in 2011, so did the demand for US goods. While US companies and government officials remain optimistic, the slowing Chinese economy makes it much more difficult for the Obama administration to meet export goals.

The slowing economies of China and other emerging nations are stunting foreign demand for U.S. goods, jeopardizing one of the Obama administration's most ambitious economic initiatives.

In his 2010 State of the Union address, President [Barack] Obama set a goal to double U.S. exports in five years—from $1.58 trillion in 2009 to $3.15 trillion by the end of 2014. With the world coming out of recession then, exports rebounded strongly at first—soaring 16.7% in 2010 and nearly 15% last year to $2.1 trillion, putting the U.S. ahead of schedule in meeting its goal.

A growing number of economists and trade experts say that performance is unlikely to be matched this year—or next [2012 and 2013]—with much of Europe in a mild recession and two of the world's largest emerging economies, China and India, decelerating from a torrid pace of double-digit annual expansion.

The doubling of U.S. exports was "an aspiration when it was disclosed, and now it seems an increasingly difficult objective to meet," says Eswar Prasad, Cornell University senior professor of trade policy.

Exports are a key driver of the American economy, accounting for more than half its expansion last year. For every $1 billion of U.S. goods or services sold overseas, about 7,000 American jobs are created, estimates Gary Hufbauer, a senior fellow at the Peterson Institute for International Economics.

U.S. exports to China . . . have already decelerated from as high as 30% year-over-year growth rates in early 2011 to the single digits at the end of the year.

Driving exports is "just one component of growing an even healthier economy," says Francisco Sanchez, U.S. undersecretary of Commerce for international trade. With 95% of the world's consumers outside the U.S., "it would be a wasted opportunity not to promote our goods and services" overseas.

Yet U.S. export growth could slow to 5% this year, and then climb to 7.5% or 8% for the next two years, predicts Gregory Daco, principal U.S. economist for IHS Global Insight. To meet its goal, the U.S. needs about twice that growth rate—an average annual rise of 14.4% in exports—for each of the next three years.

U.S. exports to China, the largest export market outside of North America, have already decelerated from as high as 30% year-over-year growth rates in early 2011 to the single digits at the end of the year. They grew at a slower pace last year than

U.S. exports to the rest of the globe as the world's second-largest economy grappled with high inflation and the threat of a housing bubble. U.S. exports of agricultural products, computer electronics and primary metals also fell sharply to China last year, after adjusting for price increases, according to an analysis by Brookings Institution, a Washington, D.C., think tank.

As China's growing demand for goods from elsewhere in the world slips as well, that could weigh on other countries' economies, and in turn, their desire for U.S. goods. China's voracious appetite for commodities such as iron and soy has fueled economic growth in countries including Australia, Chile and Brazil.

A Chinese slowdown would "ripple through trade chains and put a squeeze on U.S. exporters, whether they ship directly to China or to other destinations," says Frederic Neumann, co-head of Asian economics for HSBC [Hong Kong Banking Service] in Hong Kong.

In the first quarter, China's economy expanded 8.1% year-over-year, its slowest rate in three years. China has also lowered its 2012 economic growth target below 8% for the first time since 2005. Emerging nations such as India, Brazil and South Africa—which, along with China, are among the "priority markets" identified by the Obama administration because of their rising demand for U.S. goods—are also paring back expectations for expansion. And the developed world is grappling with a fresh recession in Europe, a slow Japanese recovery from last year's nuclear meltdown and sluggish growth elsewhere.

Mexico and Canada remain the U.S.' largest single export destinations, while the countries within the European Union account for roughly one-fifth of U.S. exports. Yet demand for American goods is rising fastest in emerging economies. Overall, 43% of U.S. exports now go to developing countries, compared with 32% a decade ago and 36% just five years ago, according to the International Monetary Fund.

The problem is, while the U.S. needs fast-growing emerging markets in order to meet its export target, there's little that the Obama administration can do to drive such growth in these markets.

China's slowing growth is already starting to be felt across the U.S.

With the outlook for the world economy constantly changing, "It's understandable that there will be challenges ahead in meeting the ambitious goals," Sanchez says.

"However, by striving to meet this goal, we're still helping U.S. companies to increase their presence overseas, export more products, and create more jobs here at home."

"It's too early," he adds, "to declare the (export) initiative to be successful or unsuccessful."

China's cooling growth chills U.S.

China's slowing growth is already starting to be felt across the U.S.

In Oregon, goods exported to China—the state's largest market—fell about a fifth last year. State exports of electronics, agricultural products and primary metals to the country also plunged, mirroring the national trend. Other states, from Nevada to Montana and Idaho, also saw merchandise exports to China drop in 2011.

Even so, the swelling middle class in China—as well as in other emerging markets in Asia and Latin America—holds "huge opportunities" for Oregon companies, says Noah Siegel, director of international affairs in Portland Mayor Sam Adams' office.

Portland is among a small group of cities forging ties with government officials and the corporate sector in fast-growing emerging markets such as China, Brazil, Vietnam and the Philippines. Portland's thinking is that, "The more diversified our companies and our city, the less likely we are to lose employment," Siegel says.

That's also the hope for Portland shipbuilder Vigor Industrial, which has set its sights on Brazil, Chile and South Africa.

To capitalize on the boom in oil exploration, Vigor aims to export 200-foot-long vessels to Brazil that ferry people and equipment to offshore drilling platforms. It's already exporting to Chile filters that remove impurities from methane gas, which fuels generators used to make electricity. The company made the filters for a client and has looked at exporting them to South Africa as well. It also hopes to export ferries to Canada.

"Had we established export relationships prior to the worldwide recession, our (shipbuilding) division may have done better," says Vince Piscitello, vice president of business development for Vigor Industrial.

But as growth cools again in the global economy, so could demand for Vigor's vessels.

"Many of our customers transport goods. If our customers are not moving goods, then they need less repair and fewer replacement vessels," Piscitello says.

Trade disputes cause worry

Even in a roaring global economy, it can be highly challenging to sell American goods in emerging markets such as China.

For instance, the growing number of trade disputes between the U.S. and China over poultry, solar cells and other products is a "source of uncertainty," says Veronica Nigh, an economist at the American Farm Bureau. The fear is that escalating tensions could ignite a trade war that hurts manufacturers in both countries.

The U.S. buys nearly four times more from China than it sells—$399 billion compared with $104 billion in 2011—yet exports from the U.S. to China have been rising at a faster pace than the other way around, according to Alaistair Chan, a Sydney-based economist at Moody's Analytics.

Market access also remains a key issue for U.S. companies doing business in China, according to Erin Ennis, a vice president at the U.S.-China Business Council.

And Chinese companies are coming into their own, competing with American firms for business in emerging and developing markets, Neumann says.

But perhaps the biggest obstacle for U.S. companies trying to tap into China's ballooning middle class is that the economy's growth remains skewed toward investment rather than consumption of goods.

"China's growth is somewhat unbalanced, which is not good for U.S. exports," Prasad says.

2

Think Again:
American Decline

Gideon Rachman

Gideon Rachman is chief foreign affairs commentator for the Financial Times.

Because the Chinese economy is a force on the global market, it can no longer be ignored. Unlike the threat of the economies of Japan or the Soviet Union in the past, the Chinese economy has the potential to surpass that of the United States in the near future. Many commentators have promoted the idea that the Chinese economy will eventually implode. This, however, seems unlikely. While the US economy remains a powerhouse in its own right, the appeal of the American Dream seems to have diminished in recent years. Whereas America once believed its values of democracy and free markets would influence all nations, these values have been forced to compete with many other value systems throughout the global economy. Even though the United States may benefit from the growth of the Chinese economy in a number of ways, there are just as many downsides for the US economy.

"We've Heard All This About American Decline Before"

This time it's different. It's certainly true that America has been through cycles of declinism in the past. Campaigning for the presidency in 1960, John F. Kennedy complained, "American strength relative to that of the Soviet Union has been slipping, and communism has been advancing steadily in every area of the world." Ezra Vogel's *Japan as Number One* was published in 1979, heralding a decade of steadily rising paranoia about Japanese manufacturing techniques and trade policies.

In the end, of course, the Soviet and Japanese threats to American supremacy proved chimerical. So Americans can be forgiven if they greet talk of a new challenge from China as just another case of the boy who cried wolf. But a frequently overlooked fact about that fable is that the boy was eventually proved right. The wolf did arrive—and China is the wolf.

The Chinese challenge to the United States is more serious for both economic and demographic reasons. The Soviet Union collapsed because its economic system was highly inefficient, a fatal flaw that was disguised for a long time because the USSR never attempted to compete on world markets. China, by contrast, has proved its economic prowess on the global stage. Its economy has been growing at 9 to 10 percent a year, on average, for roughly three decades. It is now the world's leading exporter and its biggest manufacturer, and it is sitting on more than $2.5 trillion of foreign reserves. Chinese goods compete all over the world. This is no Soviet-style economic basket case.

Japan, of course, also experienced many years of rapid economic growth and is still an export powerhouse. But it was never a plausible candidate to be No. 1. The Japanese population is less than half that of the United States, which means that the average Japanese person would have to be more than twice as rich as the average American before Japan's economy surpassed America's. That was never going to happen. By contrast, China's population is more than four times that of the United States. The famous projection by Goldman Sachs that China's economy will be bigger than that of the United States by 2027 was made before the 2008 economic crash. At the current pace, China could be No. 1 well before then.

China's economic prowess is already allowing Beijing to challenge American influence all over the world. The Chinese are the preferred partners of many African governments and the biggest trading partner of other emerging powers, such as Brazil and South Africa. China is also stepping in to buy the bonds of financially strapped members of the eurozone, such as Greece and Portugal.

Predictions of the imminent demise of the Chinese miracle have been a regular feature of Western analysis ever since it got rolling in the late 1970s.

And China is only the largest part of a bigger story about the rise of new economic and political players. America's traditional allies in Europe—Britain, France, Italy, even Germany—are slipping down the economic ranks. New powers are on the rise: India, Brazil, Turkey. They each have their own foreign-policy preferences, which collectively constrain America's ability to shape the world. Think of how India and Brazil sided with China at the global climate-change talks. Or the votes by Turkey and Brazil against America at the United Nations on sanctions against Iran. That is just a taste of things to come.

"China Will Implode Sooner or Later"

Don't count on it. It is certainly true that when Americans are worrying about national decline, they tend to overlook the weaknesses of their scariest-looking rival. The flaws in the Soviet and Japanese systems became obvious only in retrospect. Those who are confident that American hegemony will be extended long into the future point to the potential liabilities of the Chinese system. In a recent interview with the *Times* of London, former U.S. President George W. Bush suggested that

China's internal problems mean that its economy will be unlikely to rival America's in the foreseeable future. "Do I still think America will remain the sole superpower?" he asked. "I do."

But predictions of the imminent demise of the Chinese miracle have been a regular feature of Western analysis ever since it got rolling in the late 1970s. In 1989, the Communist Party seemed to be staggering after the Tiananmen Square massacre. In the 1990s, economy watchers regularly pointed to the parlous state of Chinese banks and state-owned enterprises. Yet the Chinese economy has kept growing, doubling in size roughly every seven years.

Of course, it would be absurd to pretend that China does not face major challenges. In the short term, there is plenty of evidence that a property bubble is building in big cities like Shanghai, and inflation is on the rise. Over the long term, China has alarming political and economic transitions to navigate. The Communist Party is unlikely to be able to maintain its monopoly on political power forever. And the country's traditional dependence on exports and an undervalued currency are coming under increasing criticism from the United States and other international actors demanding a "rebalancing" of China's export-driven economy. The country also faces major demographic and environmental challenges: The population is aging rapidly as a result of the one-child policy, and China is threatened by water shortages and pollution.

Yet even if you factor in considerable future economic and political turbulence, it would be a big mistake to assume that the Chinese challenge to U.S. power will simply disappear. Once countries get the hang of economic growth, it takes a great deal to throw them off course. The analogy to the rise of Germany from the mid-19th century onward is instructive. Germany went through two catastrophic military defeats, hyperinflation, the Great Depression, the collapse of democracy, and the destruction of its major cities and infrastructure by

Allied bombs. And yet by the end of the 1950s, West Germany was once again one of the world's leading economies, albeit shorn of its imperial ambitions.

America's appeal might also diminish if the country is no longer so closely associated with opportunity, prosperity, and success.

In a nuclear age, China is unlikely to get sucked into a world war, so it will not face turbulence and disorder on remotely the scale Germany did in the 20th century. And whatever economic and political difficulties it does experience will not be enough to stop the country's rise to great-power status. Sheer size and economic momentum mean that the Chinese juggernaut will keep rolling forward, no matter what obstacles lie in its path.

"America Still Leads Across the Board"

For now. As things stand, America has the world's largest economy, the world's leading universities, and many of its biggest companies. The U.S. military is also incomparably more powerful than any rival. The United States spends almost as much on its military as the rest of the world put together. And let's also add in America's intangible assets. The country's combination of entrepreneurial flair and technological prowess has allowed it to lead the technological revolution. Talented immigrants still flock to U.S. shores. And now that Barack Obama is in the White House, the country's soft power has received a big boost. For all his troubles, polls show Obama is still the most charismatic leader in the world; Hu Jintao doesn't even come close. America also boasts the global allure of its creative industries (Hollywood and all that), its values, the increasing universality of the English language, and the attractiveness of the American Dream.

All true—but all more vulnerable than you might think. American universities remain a formidable asset. But if the U.S. economy is not generating jobs, then those bright Asian graduate students who fill up the engineering and computer-science departments at Stanford University and MIT will return home in larger numbers. *Fortune's* latest ranking of the world's largest companies has only two American firms in the top 10—Walmart at No. 1 and ExxonMobil at No. 3. There are already three Chinese firms in the top 10: Sinopec, State Grid, and China National Petroleum. America's appeal might also diminish if the country is no longer so closely associated with opportunity, prosperity, and success. And though many foreigners are deeply attracted to the American Dream, there is also a deep well of anti-American sentiment in the world that al Qaeda and others have skillfully exploited, Obama or no Obama.

As for the U.S. military, the lesson of the Iraq and Afghan wars is that America's martial prowess is less useful than former Defense Secretary Donald Rumsfeld and others imagined. U.S. troops, planes, and missiles can overthrow a government on the other side of the world in weeks, but pacifying and stabilizing a conquered country is another matter. Years after apparent victory, America is still bogged down by an apparently endless insurgency in Afghanistan.

Not only are Americans losing their appetite for foreign adventures, but the U.S. military budget is clearly going to come under pressure in this new age of austerity. The present paralysis in Washington offers little hope that the United States will deal with its budgetary problems swiftly or efficiently. The U.S. government's continuing reliance on foreign lending makes the country vulnerable, as Secretary of State Hillary Clinton's humbling 2009 request to the Chinese to keep buying U.S. Treasury bills revealed. America is funding its military supremacy through deficit spending, meaning the war in Afghanistan is effectively being paid for with a Chinese credit card. Little wonder that Adm. Mike Mullen, chairman of the Joint Chiefs of Staff, has identified the burgeoning national debt as the single largest threat to U.S. national security.

Meanwhile, China's spending on its military continues to grow rapidly. The country will soon announce the construction of its first aircraft carrier and is aiming to build five or six in total. Perhaps more seriously, China's development of new missile and anti-satellite technology threatens the command of the sea and skies on which the United States bases its Pacific supremacy. In a nuclear age, the U.S. and Chinese militaries are unlikely to clash. A common Chinese view is that the United States will instead eventually find it can no longer afford its military position in the Pacific. U.S. allies in the region—Japan, South Korea, and increasingly India—may partner more with Washington to try to counter rising Chinese power. But if the United States has to scale back its presence in the Pacific for budgetary reasons, its allies will start to accommodate themselves to a rising China. Beijing's influence will expand, and the Asia-Pacific region—the emerging center of the global economy—will become China's backyard.

"Globalization Is Bending the World the Way of the West"

Not really. One reason why the United States was relaxed about China's rise in the years after the end of the Cold War was the deeply ingrained belief that globalization was spreading Western values. Some even thought that globalization and Americanization were virtually synonymous.

Pundit Fareed Zakaria was prescient when he wrote that the "rise of the rest" (i.e., non-American powers) would be one of the major features of a "post-American world." But even Zakaria argued that this trend was essentially beneficial to the United States: "The power shift . . . is good for America, if approached properly. The world is going America's way. Countries are becoming more open, market-friendly, and democratic."

Both former [Presidents] George W. Bush and Bill Clinton took a similar view that globalization and free trade would serve as a vehicle for the export of American values. In 1999, two years before China's accession to the World Trade Organization, Bush argued, "Economic freedom creates habits of liberty. And habits of liberty create expectations of democracy.... Trade freely with China, and time is on our side."

It is now entirely conceivable that when China becomes the world's largest economy—let us say in 2027—it will still be a one-party state run by the Communist Party.

There were two important misunderstandings buried in this theorizing. The first was that economic growth would inevitably—and fairly swiftly—lead to democratization. The second was that new democracies would inevitably be more friendly and helpful toward the United States. Neither assumption is working out.

In 1989, after the Tiananmen Square massacre, few Western analysts would have believed that 20 years later China would still be a one-party state—and that its economy would also still be growing at phenomenal rates. The common (and comforting) Western assumption was that China would have to choose between political liberalization and economic failure. Surely a tightly controlled one-party state could not succeed in the era of cell phones and the World Wide Web? As Clinton put it during a visit to China in 1998, "In this global information age, when economic success is built on ideas, personal freedom is ... essential to the greatness of any modern nation."

In fact, China managed to combine censorship and one-party rule with continuing economic success over the follow-

ing decade. The confrontation between the Chinese government and Google in 2010 was instructive. Google, that icon of
the digital era, threatened to withdraw from China in protest
at censorship, but it eventually backed down in return for to-
ken concessions. It is now entirely conceivable that when
China becomes the world's largest economy—let us say in
2027—it will still be a one-party state run by the Communist
Party.

And even if China does democratize, there is absolutely no
guarantee that this will make life easier for the United States,
let alone prolong America's global hegemony. The idea that
democracies are liable to agree on the big global issues is now
being undermined on a regular basis. India does not agree
with the United States on climate change or the Doha round
of trade talks. Brazil does not agree with the United States on
how to handle Venezuela or Iran. A more democratic Turkey
is today also a more Islamist Turkey, which is now refusing to
take the American line on either Israel or Iran. In a similar
vein, a more democratic China might also be a more prickly
China, if the popularity of nationalist books and Internet sites
in the Middle Kingdom is any guide.

"Globalization Is Not a Zero-Sum Game"

Don't be too sure. Successive U.S. presidents, from the first
[George] Bush to [Barack] Obama, have explicitly welcomed
China's rise. Just before his first visit to China, Obama sum-
marized the traditional approach when he said, "Power does
not need to be a zero-sum game, and nations need not fear
the success of another. . . . We welcome China's efforts to play
a greater role on the world stage."

But whatever they say in formal speeches, America's leaders are clearly beginning to have their doubts, and rightly so.
It is a central tenet of modern economics that trade is mutually beneficial for both partners, a win-win rather than a zero-
sum. But that implies the rules of the game aren't rigged.

Speaking before the 2010 World Economic Forum, Larry Summers, then Obama's chief economic advisor, remarked pointedly that the normal rules about the mutual benefits of trade do not necessarily apply when one trading partner is practicing mercantilist or protectionist policies. The U.S. government clearly thinks that China's undervaluation of its currency is a form of protectionism that has led to global economic imbalances and job losses in the United States. Leading economists, such as *New York Times* columnist Paul Krugman and the Peterson Institute's C. Fred Bergsten, have taken a similar line, arguing that tariffs or other retaliatory measures would be a legitimate response. So much for the win-win world.

Growing Chinese economic and military clout clearly poses a long-term threat to American hegemony in the Pacific.

And when it comes to the broader geopolitical picture, the world of the future looks even more like a zero-sum game, despite the gauzy rhetoric of globalization that comforted the last generation of American politicians. For the United States has been acting as if the mutual interests created by globalization have repealed one of the oldest laws of international politics: the notion that rising players eventually clash with established powers.

In fact, rivalry between a rising China and a weakened America is now apparent across a whole range of issues, from territorial disputes in Asia to human rights. It is mercifully unlikely that the United States and China would ever actually go to war, but that is because both sides have nuclear weapons, not because globalization has magically dissolved their differences.

At the G-20 [finance ministers and central bank governors from the twenty major economies] summit in November [2010], the U.S. drive to deal with "global economic imbalances" was essentially thwarted by China's obdurate refusal to change its currency policy. The 2009 climate-change talks in Copenhagen ended in disarray after another U.S.-China stand-off. Growing Chinese economic and military clout clearly poses a long-term threat to American hegemony in the Pacific. The Chinese reluctantly agreed to a new package of U.N. sanctions on Iran, but the cost of securing Chinese agreement was a weak deal that is unlikely to derail the Iranian nuclear program. Both sides have taken part in the talks with North Korea, but a barely submerged rivalry prevents truly effective Sino-American cooperation. China does not like Kim Jong Il's regime, but it is also very wary of a reunified Korea on its borders, particularly if the new Korea still played host to U.S. troops. China is also competing fiercely for access to resources, in particular oil, which is driving up global prices.

American leaders are right to reject zero-sum logic in public. To do anything else would needlessly antagonize the Chinese. But that shouldn't obscure this unavoidable fact: As economic and political power moves from West to East, new international rivalries are inevitably emerging.

The United States still has formidable strengths. Its economy will eventually recover. Its military has a global presence and a technological edge that no other country can yet match. But America will never again experience the global dominance it enjoyed in the 17 years between the Soviet Union's collapse in 1991 and the financial crisis of 2008. Those days are over.

3

Black Markets Offer the Chinese Economy an Advantage

Bradley Gardner

Bradley Gardner is a business writer based in Beijing.

While the Chinese central government is often given credit for the country's economic growth, private enterprise in cities like Wenzhou play a larger role than previously acknowledged. Wenzhou's distance from the official government in China allowed many entrepreneurs to develop a different business model, one based on an underground financial system. The private sector, then, is partly responsible for the success of the Chinese economy. Likewise, the Wenzhou model has been exported by the Wenzhounese to other countries and to other regions of China. While there is always a danger of a government crackdown in Wenzhou, the global reach of Chinese capitalism promises even greater economic returns in the future.

Chen Mingyuan has lived here all his life, but he still gets lost every time he drives into Wenzhou. "All the roads in this town were built by businessmen, so none of them make any sense," Chen says as we back out of what we just discovered is a one-way street. For the last 30 years, private citizens in this southeastern China metropolis have largely taken over one of the least questioned prerogatives of governments the world over: infrastructure.

Driving down the cluttered and half-constructed streets of this 3-million-strong boomtown requires frequent U-turns and the patience of Buddha, but every road eventually leads back to a factory. Each factory is in turn surrounded by a maze of roads filled with hundreds of small feeder shops selling spare parts, building materials, and scraps. Every haphazard street in this town seems to have an economic purpose.

We are driving to see Cai Shuxian, the manager and majority owner of a clothing factory in which Chen owns a 10 percent stake. Cai, a lightly built 32-year-old, is typical of the entrepreneurs who have made it big during Wenzhou's three-decade boom, vaulting from shop-floor grunt to factory owner in a dizzyingly short period of time. "We earned very little in those days," the high-school dropout recalls of his first job, "about 600 yuan [roughly $100] a month." Within six years Cai was able to leverage his money and know-how into building a factory of his own, which now employs more than 100 people.

Cai glides over the source of his start-up capital, although it definitely was not one of China's state-owned banks. "Banks only give you money when you don't need it," he says. He explains that during the 2009 financial crisis, when banks were aggressively lending as a form of stimulus, people would reinvest the money in Wenzhou's underground financial system, where deposit interest rates are higher than the official lending rate.

The Chinese say that in this region [Wenzhou] "the mountains are high and the emperor is far away"—in other words, the government isn't paying much attention.

Cai says his Horatio Alger story is "typical of Wenzhou." And it is. Only a few days later I am introduced to the manager of a factory making transmissions for South Korean cars. Although he had the advantage of finishing high school, his starting salary wasn't any higher. Cai's dismissive attitude toward the government is also typical. Wenzhou has become one of the richest cities in China under a regulatory regime that borders on anarchism.

The Wenzhou Model

Foreign businessmen, politicians, and journalists who fly into Beijing or Shanghai often get the impression that the Chinese government is the main driver behind the jaw-dropping development of what was until recently one of the worst large economies in the world. In Shanghai you fly to a state-built airport, ride on a state-built maglev train through the Pudong district, and behold a city of skyscrapers that appeared out of nowhere a little more than a decade ago with the help of generous government subsidies and investment from state-owned enterprises. Whatever local company you're interested in, chances are the government is interested in it as well.

In southern China, things look rather different. The Chinese say that in this region "the mountains are high and the emperor is far away"—in other words, the government isn't paying much attention. Companies are mainly small or medium-sized enterprises, government services are slight, and laws are routinely ignored. According to official statistics, the three southern coastal provinces of Zhejiang, Guangdong, and Fujian have the first, second, and fourth wealthiest citizens, respectively, in the country. They are the center of China's export sector and the primary destination for China's millions of internal economic migrants. Here is where the real Chinese miracle is happening.

The city and region of Wenzhou play an important role in this story. The Wenzhounese have a reputation for both an uncanny sense of business and an almost pathological disregard for the government. The mountains here are no metaphor: Seventy-eight percent of the Wenzhou prefecture is covered by mountains, a fact that proved pivotal to the area's early development and the central government's response to it.

In 1978, when China's economic reforms were just being launched, Wenzhou was extremely poor, about 90 percent rural, with smaller land allocations than other areas and poor connections to larger markets. Even today, the vast majority of local entrepreneurs have less than eight years of formal education, and the current population of foreigners is estimated at only a couple of hundred. The Wenzhounese government received directives from Beijing but found that without accompanying support they lacked resources to run the economy by diktat [harsh penalty]. Fortunately, a central government that wasn't offering much support also wasn't paying much attention.

Although bureaucrats still occasionally try to impose state controls on the city, the futility of the effort quickly becomes apparent.

So private citizens quietly took over many of the services that elsewhere are either provided or heavily regulated by the state. Local authorities, lacking other options, didn't try to stop them. The most important development in those early days was the city's flourishing underground financial system, which according to the local branch of the People's Bank of China (China's central bank) currently is used by 89 percent of Wenzhounese private citizens and 57 percent of local companies.

The Effective Private Sector

More dramatically, private citizens were the first to connect Wenzhou to neighboring regions by building roads, bridges, and highways, as well as the city's airports and substantial portions of the dock. Even today the city is scattered with infrastructure investment firms through which groups of businessmen pool money to build the transport routes they all need to get their goods from factory to the point of sale. The result is not pretty. Aside from the confusion faced even by residents driving into the city, it is not uncommon to see sidewalks torn up to insert piping, with seemingly no intention of replacing the concrete. Nevertheless, the system is crudely efficient, merchants can all easily access factories, and the factories in this geographically isolated city now have sales networks that span the globe.

The government's indifference didn't last forever. But when the authorities got around to paying attention, they decided not to mess with a good thing. In 1985 *Liberation Daily*, a paper sponsored by the Shanghai Communist Party, referred to Wenzhou as a "model" for other parts of China to study. In the next year 15,000 government officials visited the city to learn, not crack down. Although bureaucrats still occasionally try to impose state controls on the city, the futility of the effort quickly becomes apparent. By now the local Chamber of Commerce has taken to negotiating trade deals both domestically and internationally because, as in most other things, the private sector is more effective here.

Wenzhou is the center of China's light manufacturing empire and the richest city in China's richest province. (Nationwide, Shenzhen, Shanghai, and Guangzhou narrowly edge out Wenzhou—in the official figures, at least.) A quick walk down a Wenzhou street reveals a bewildering display of commerce. The streets around the railway station are covered in stalls selling $3 blue jeans and $5 boots. There's a city block dedicated to baby clothes next to a street that sells plastic signs for bathroom doors. In one run-down alleyway you'll see people repairing televisions, making blankets, and selling fruits, vegetables, and poultry (live or dead). Further outside the center, you can find small shops dedicated to aluminum rods, sheet metal, tire rims, and tires.

Much of this low-level commerce depends on the same official negligence that fuels the factories. Pool halls are set up wherever there's open space that you can set a tarp over. Gambling dens are openly advertised. Taxi drivers often drive off the meter. The karaoke parlors are numerous, and almost all of them double as brothels. The poorest residents take part in one of the largest citizen recycling programs anywhere in the world. In an alley one family collects scraps of fabric to sell to the local textile mills, another hoards scraps of paper and cardboard to send to the paper mills, and in front of a lot that looks like it is being used for a garbage dump, a man has set up a secondhand goods shop.

Wenzhou was one of the first cities to develop methods to work around the financial sector's aversion to private enterprise.

Unskilled workers in Wenzhou are paid one of the highest wages in the country, roughly $380 a month according to official figures (even higher—between $450 and $600—according to entrepreneurs' estimates). It is here that people like Cai make their fortune.

Medicis on the Yellow Sea

China's formal financial system generally disfavors lending to smaller companies. Interest rates are capped, state institutions come with a government guarantee, and Beijing regularly issues lending decrees, all of which make banks reluctant to throw money at small, private actors with poor or nonexistent credit histories.

Wenzhou was one of the first cities to develop methods to work around the financial sector's aversion to private enterprise. According to local entrepreneurs, it was this secondary banking system that made the biggest contribution to Wenzhou's early development. "While northern people kept the money they made, Wenzhou people immediately lent it to their friends to help get ventures off the ground," says Weng Yuwen, a Wenzhou native now running a clothing design company out of nearby Hangzhou.

Dozens of financing options are available, and although most of them intrude on the jurisdiction of the state-controlled banking system, they are not all illegal. Or at least not completely illegal. The different levels of legality that Wenzhounese perceive are a bit of a puzzle to an outside observer. Weng quickly disavows any knowledge of "underground banking"; like every other Wenzhou entrepreneur I speak to, he has "friends" who have dealt with gray-market lenders but declares he would never do so himself. A more standard form of getting a loan, he explains, is borrowing from a contact . . . who also happens to be lending to a large number of other entrepreneurs at interest. Weng contemplates this arrangement, then admits that the whole thing might be "somewhat illegal."

Gray-market lenders are often established, though technically illegal, financial institutions that lend primarily working-capital loans at rates as high as 10 percent a month. Contacts often modify interest rates based on how well you know them. Forms of repayment enforcement differ. Weng points out that in a community so dependent on *guanxi*—relationships— defaulting on a contact's loan could blackball you from future business opportunities. Weng doesn't clarify how defaulters are treated by underground debt collectors, but he does say they "aren't the type of people I'd want to get involved with."

Lending also takes place through a number of formal lending institutions that have become informal depositing institutions. Pawnshops in Wenzhou are very different from those in the West. The shops can give out loans of millions of dollars backed by property and stocks, and they can pay depositors interest rates three to four percentage points higher than the official lending rate at banks. Similarly, credit guarantee institutions, which were originally set up to co-sign on riskier bank loans to small private firms, eventually began lending their own (or depositors') money. These institutions are essentially legal, however, because they call their depositors "investors."

Degrees of Legality

As Wenzhounese have become more wealthy, they have found it easier to operate within the formal financial system, although they still frequently subvert state intentions. Every wealthy Wenzhounese I interview, for instance, boasts of owning five to six apartments. Part of the motivation for these purchases is the high return on real estate in China, but the other major reason is that remortgaging real estate is a relatively easy source of capital in both the formal and informal banking systems.

Corruption is particularly commonplace in the prefectural taxation bureau, an agency that has been asserting more control over the local economy.

The Wenzhounese are also well aware that government support is a ticket to greater banking support—and doesn't come with significant oversight—so they will often raise funds with state-owned enterprises in order to get support for projects that are not always completed in the form originally planned. "It helps being from Wenzhou," says Weng, because "people just assume that Wenzhounese have the resources to complete the projects they're pitching."

By far the most common form of start-up financing is something akin to venture capital: investing in an entrepreneur's project on the hope he will eventually buy you out with a decent return. This approach also is used to manipulate the banking system. Once you get your business up and running, it is much easier to get loans to buy your investor out.

Although Wenzhounese quibble about degrees of illegality, there is no question that stepping over the line can lead to serious consequences. In April, Wu Ying, a 29-year-old Wenzhou woman, was sentenced to death for illegal fund raising. The case touched a nerve, with numerous articles published supporting Wu in the Chinese media, because none of the public evidence pointed to anything out of the ordinary about her actions—except perhaps the 80 percent returns she was offering investors, and the similar interest rates she charged on loans, which led some to suggest her mistake was lending to someone with political connections.

State Interference

In Wenzhou local commercial institutions generally have more representative power than the local government. The Chamber of Commerce has been known to independently approach government delegations with potential investment opportunities—or challenges to trade sanctions—without consulting the Chinese state.

Local officials, by contrast, are notorious for graft, especially through land sales. The party chairman of one Wenzhou district refused to return from France after being indicted in 2008. Internet vigilantes at 703804.com have taken to tracking down individuals who have fled after embezzling funds.

Corruption is particularly commonplace in the prefectural taxation bureau, an agency that has been asserting more control over the local economy. "In the '90s paying taxes wasn't that important," says one Wenzhou entrepreneur, "but these days you can't avoid it." Despite having one of the highest corporate tax rates in the world, however, China has a very generous deduction scheme, and if you have friends in the taxation bureau, the same entrepreneur says, "you don't have to file all the paperwork."

I see this process up close when I interview the head of an auto parts factory over dinner. Several of his friends are present, the beer and Baijiu rice liquor are flowing freely, and the food is far more than all of us could eat. Halfway through the dinner, three members of the local taxation bureau join us. The factory owner introduces them as friends and proceeds to treat them on his tab. Afterwards he takes the officials to a local karaoke bar to meet prostitutes.

A Permissive Government

The Wenzhounese have mixed feelings about this situation. As the factory owner's friend escorts me back to my hotel, he adopts a cynical look and says, "People do business differently here." But later, when I describe the scene to Weng, he shrugs. "It's the same all over the world," he says. "People who have good relationships are more successful in business."

The government may not allow Wenzhounese to invest freely abroad, but they do it anyway.

The local government has helped Wenzhou enormously in one area: protecting the city from more distant levels of government. Even during the Cultural Revolution, authorities were relatively permissive toward private business, and they defended the city against conservative attacks in the 1980s. Many entrepreneurs acknowledge that local leaders' laxity is deliberate. "Hangzhou has a good government: They ignore you unless you're making more than [Renminbi] RMB 10 million [$1.5 million]," says Weng. "In Wenzhou you can make twice as much, and they'll still ignore you."

A sign of how much the city government has internalized the local business culture came last January, when the Wenzhou foreign trade and economic cooperation bureau began a pilot program to allow Wenzhou residents to invest up to $200 million a year abroad. The program was canceled a week later because local officials had forgotten to run the idea by Beijing.

Spreading the Wenzhou Model

The government may not allow Wenzhounese to invest freely abroad, but they do it anyway. Across continental Europe and in much of the emerging world, people from Wenzhou are by far the largest component of the Chinese diaspora. Wenzhounese make up the majority of Chinese restaurant owners from Madrid to Vienna, and in some places they have recreated the Wenzhou experience on European soil.

In no place is this more true than in Prato, Italy, near Florence, where 12,000 of the city's population of 188,000 are legal Chinese residents, mostly from Wenzhou. The local government estimates that there are 10,000 more illegal Wenzhou residents, while estimates from the right-wing party that runs the city reach 35,000. Forty percent of local businesses are owned by Chinese.

Many of Wenzhou's business practices have carried over from China, although Italians disagree about how much lawbreaking is going on. According to Prato Mayor Roberto Cenni, between January and May 2010 police carried out 152 inspections on Chinese-owned premises, resulting in 152 penalties. The region also has the highest level of tax evasion in Tuscany, according to Vinicio Bacio of Invitalia, the Italian investment promotion agency, although he argues that the situation is getting under control. "While there is still a large quantity of activities undeclared," Bacio says, "most of the manufacturing and trade promoted by the Chinese community in the textile area is regularly reported."

A reputation for poor quality has made it just as hard to sell Chinese goods for high margins in China as abroad.

Despite a campaign by Mayor Cenni to crack down on Wenzhou business, Bacio notes that the Chinese presence has revitalized the local textile industry, which had long been in decline. "The relationships [between Wenzhounese and Italian factories] are closer than what it appears externally," notes Bacio, with contracts, supplies, and investment crossing over between the two communities.

Global Reach

The global reach of Wenzhou entrepreneurs, combined with their liberalized financial system, has made the local community much more attuned to international supply and demand and much more able to transfer capacity to the appropriate regions. Weng's clothing business is one example. The company employs 60 people, with designers getting paid between [Renminbi] RMB 10,000 to RMB 30,000 ($1,500 to $4,500) per month. The latter amount is an almost unheard of salary in China. Weng outsources all of his factory work to about 30 different factories in three neighboring provinces, and those factories often outsource to others that produce even more cheaply. Weng has heard of many Wenzhounese moving production to Southeast Asia, although he says his company isn't big enough to make the shipping worth it.

Weng and Cai both produce solely for the Chinese market. "There is so much untapped demand here that there's absolutely no need to export," says Weng. A reputation for poor quality has made it just as hard to sell Chinese goods for high margins in China as abroad, so the Wenzhounese are making concerted efforts to market themselves and China as a whole.

The Wenzhou store for JNBY, a local clothing brand that has successfully expanded globally, features a poster of a white woman proudly holding a sign declaring "Made in China." Cai sends all his designers on trips to Italy twice a year to study Italian fashions.

Local businesses have also been looking toward emerging markets. The Wenzhounese population of Dubai is significant, which is no surprise given that the city, with its "Dragon Mart" selling a variety of low-cost goods from China, has become a staging point for trade across the Middle East and Africa. Chinese textiles have taken over the South African market, as have Chinese plastic goods in Egypt. Both are mainstays of the Wenzhou economy.

Perhaps more important, the Wenzhounese have become untethered from their city of origin. Wenzhounese businessmen seem to take credit for every private-sector industry in China, from coal mines in northern China to cell phone factories in southern China, and they always seem to have a few friends in the business to back up their claims.

These investments across China are bringing not only Wenzhounese money but the Wenzhounese way of doing business to obscure parts of the country. The future of Wenzhou will now lie in providing services to these less developed areas, argues one button and zipper factory owner. What sort of services? "Finance, karaoke parlors, that sort of thing," he says. It doesn't seem to occur to him that all the services he mentions are technically illegal.

4

US Agriculture Exports to China Benefit the US Economy

Gregory Meyer and Leslie Hook

Gregory Meyer is a New York correspondent and Leslie Hook is a Beijing correspondent for the Financial Times.

The growth of the Chinese economy has allowed American farmers to increase exports over recent years. In particular, the export of soybeans and cotton has helped reduce US trade deficits with China. While trade restrictions in China on beef and other US agriculture goods have created tensions, US farmers overall seem to have a bright export future with Chinese markets.

The concrete silos of the first US grain export depot to be built in 25 years are rising 66 miles up river from the Pacific Ocean, two mountain ranges and more than 1,500 miles away from the nation's midwestern breadbasket.

The location is easily explained: traders who historically barged most of the US grain surplus to the Gulf of Mexico now want to be closer to Asia. "China is the major driver," says Larry Clarke, chief executive of the joint venture of commodity traders Bunge and Itochu and South Korean shipowner STX Pan Ocean that is developing the $200m [million] (€159m, £133m) terminal in Washington state.

As US politicians lose sleep over the trade deficit with China and the dollar-renminbi exchange rate, American farmers are eyeing a record $14bn [billion] in exports there this year. The US had a $4bn trade surplus in agricultural products with China in the first four months of 2010, helping shave the total deficit to $71bn in the period. . . .

Agricultural exports to Asia are reshaping the US logistics landscape. The new Port of Longview grain terminal will handle 8m tonnes a year. At nearby Port of Grays Harbor a midwestern soyabean co-operative is adding storage for 50,000 tonnes of grain.

The US is the world's largest exporter of soyabeans and cotton, commodities for which China is the world's top importer.

Down the coast, California has surpassed New Orleans as the top point of departure for US cotton shipments, "given the Asian orientation of exports", according to a report prepared for the ICE Futures exchange [Intercontinental Exchange]. At the port of South Louisiana on the Gulf of Mexico, still North America's leading grain export hub, China last year blew past Japan to become the top destination for outbound bulk tonnage.

Ken O'Hollaren, executive director at the Port of Longview, says the grain project there will employ 50 permanent workers. "Clearly, the growth market they had in mind to accommodate was the China market," he said.

US Agriculture Exports to China

The US is the world's largest exporter of soyabeans and cotton, commodities for which China is the world's top importer. Exports "exploded" after China's 2001 accession to the World Trade Organisation, says the US Department of Agriculture. Growing livestock and textile industries have stoked demand for animal feed and fibres. "It's huge," says Randy Mann, who cultivates corn, soyabeans and wheat on 2,500 acres (1,000 hectares) in Kentucky and chairs a trade and international affairs committee of the American Soyabean Association. "Probably a third of the price on the Chicago Board of Trade is related to the soyabean market in China. That's the impact it can have." Soyabean prices have doubled in a decade to $10 a bushel.

US agricultural exports to China are a relative bright spot in the trade relationship, despite some tensions over farm products. US beef is banned in China over BSE [Bovine Spongiform Encephalopathy] fears dating from 2003, for example, and US chicken imports face high antidumping and antisubsidy duties. Dairy is also an area of concern, with the countries currently negotiating over a new certification requirement for US dairy imports.

But there are few non-tariff barriers on products like soyabeans and cotton. China has approved genetically modified soyabeans from the US, for example, and does not cap imports.

US politicians say China could do more to let in foreign agriculture. The US International Trade Commission is investigating complaints that imports are limited to a few products. "We face unjustified restrictions in the Chinese market," says Max Baucus, the Montana Democrat who chairs the Senate finance committee. Barack Obama, US president, last week named Patricia Woertz, head of Archer Daniels Midland, an Illinois-based grain trading and processing company, to a council formed to invigorate US exports.

The Chinese government has made self-sufficiency in agricultural production a national goal, and China typically produces enough wheat, rice and corn to meet domestic demand. This year, for the first time in 15 years, US corn was shipped to China after a poor domestic crop last season, though total import volumes are small.

China's agricultural production is constrained by shrinking arable land area, limited water supply, outdated technology and small plot sizes. The median Chinese farm plot is less than one acre, preventing economies of scale. China uses subsidies and price supports to farmers to remain nearly self-sufficient in wheat, the USDA [United States Department of Agriculture] says.

"Past liberalisation of policies for formerly strategic crops, such as soyabeans and cotton, indicates that China is willing to forgo self-sufficiency when costs are high and the crop is not 'too strategic,'" the USDA said in a recent report.

Liberalisation has not moved fast enough for some. At a trade commission hearing last month, US potato farmers claimed that China showed a "willingness to use quarantine matters politically" as it keeps out American tubers.

5

Manufacturing in China Remains a Threat to US Jobs

Economist

The Economist *is a weekly international news and business publication located in London.*

As labor costs have soared in China, many experts have predicted the end of outsourcing to the country by US manufacturers. However, despite this change, China retains a strong manufacturing advantage. China's large population is a potent resource for both workers and consumers, and Chinese manufacturers have grown more efficient and reliable. Although the cost of manufacturing in China has increased, the country will remain an important global player in the near future.

Travel by ferry from Hong Kong to Shenzhen, in one of the regions that makes China the workshop of the world, and an enormous billboard greets you: "Time is Money, Efficiency is Life".

China is the world's largest manufacturing power. Its output of televisions, smartphones, steel pipes and other things you can drop on your foot surpassed America's in 2010. China now accounts for a fifth of global manufacturing. Its factories have made so much, so cheaply that they have curbed inflation in many of its trading partners. But the era of cheap China may be drawing to a close.

Rising Manufacturing Costs in China

Costs are soaring, starting in the coastal provinces where factories have historically clustered. Increases in land prices, environmental and safety regulations and taxes all play a part. The biggest factor, though, is labour.

On March 5th Standard Chartered, an investment bank, released a survey of over 200 Hong Kong-based manufacturers operating in the Pearl River Delta. It found that wages have already risen by 10% this year. Foxconn, a Taiwanese contract manufacturer that makes Apple's iPads (and much more besides) in Shenzhen, put up salaries by 16–25% last month.

"It's not cheap like it used to be," laments Dale Weathington of Kolcraft, an American firm that uses contract manufacturers to make prams in southern China. Labour costs have surged by 20% a year for the past four years, he grumbles. China's coastal provinces are losing their power to suck workers out of the hinterland. These migrant workers often go home during the Chinese New Year break. In previous years 95% of Mr Weathington's staff returned. This year only 85% did.

If cheap China is fading, what will replace it? Will factories shift to poorer countries with cheaper labour? That is the conventional wisdom, but it is wrong.

Kolcraft's experience is typical. When the American Chamber of Commerce in Shanghai asked its members recently about their biggest challenges, 91% mentioned "rising costs". Corruption and piracy were far behind. Labour costs (including benefits) for blue-collar workers in Guangdong rose by 12% a year, in dollar terms, from 2002 to 2009; in Shanghai, 14% a year. Roland Berger, a consultancy, reckons the comparable figure was only 8% in the Philippines and 1% in Mexico.

Joerg Wuttke, a veteran industrialist with the EU [European Union] Chamber of Commerce in China, predicts that the cost to manufacture in China could soar twofold or even threefold by 2020. AlixPartners, a consultancy, offers this intriguing extrapolation: if China's currency and shipping costs were to rise by 5% annually and wages were to go up by 30% a year, by 2015 it would be just as cheap to make things in North America as to make them in China and ship them there. In reality, the convergence will probably be slower. But the trend is clear.

If cheap China is fading, what will replace it? Will factories shift to poorer countries with cheaper labour? That is the conventional wisdom, but it is wrong.

Chinese workers are paid more because they are producing more.

Advantage China

Brian Noll of PPC, which makes connectors for televisions, says his firm seriously considered moving its operations to Vietnam. Labour was cheaper there, but Vietnam lacked reliable suppliers of services such as nickel plating, heat treatment and special stamping. In the end, PPC decided not to leave China. Instead, it is automating more processes in its factory near Shanghai, replacing some (but not all) workers with machines.

Labour costs are often 30% lower in countries other than China, says John Rice, GE's [General Electric] vice chairman, but this is typically more than offset by other problems, especially the lack of a reliable supply chain. GE did open a new plant in Vietnam to make wind turbines, but Mr Rice insists that talent was the lure, not cheap labour. Thanks to a big government shipyard nearby, his plant was able to hire world-class welders. Except in commodity businesses, "competence will always trump cost," he says.

Sunil Gidumal, a Hong Kong-based entrepreneur, makes tin boxes that Harrods, Marks & Spencer and other retailers use to hold biscuits. Wages, which make up a third of his costs, have doubled in the past four years at his factories in Guangdong. Workers in Sri Lanka are 35–40% cheaper, he says, but he finds them less efficient. So he is keeping a smaller factory in China to serve America and China's domestic market. Only the tins bound for Europe are made in Sri Lanka, since shipping costs are lower than from China.

Louis Kuijs of the Fung Global Institute, a think-tank, observes that some low-tech, labour-intensive industries, such as T-shirts and cheap trainers, have already left China. And some firms are employing a "China + 1" strategy, opening just one factory in another country to test the waters and provide a back-up.

Economic Growth in China

But coastal China has enduring strengths, despite soaring costs. First, it is close to the booming Chinese domestic market. This is a huge advantage. No other country has so many newly pecunious consumers clamouring for stuff.

Second, Chinese wages may be rising fast, but so is Chinese productivity. The precise numbers are disputed, but the trend is not. Chinese workers are paid more because they are producing more.

Third, China is huge. Its labour pool is large and flexible enough to accommodate seasonal industries that make Christmas lights or toys, says Ivo Naumann of AlixPartners. In response to sudden demand, a Chinese factory making iPhones was able to rouse 8,000 workers from their dormitory and put them on the assembly line at midnight, according to the *New York Times*. Not the next day. Midnight. Nowhere else are such feats feasible.

Fourth, China's supply chain is sophisticated and supple. Professor Zheng Yusheng of the Cheung Kong Graduate

School of Business argues that the right way to measure manufacturing competitiveness is not by comparing labour costs alone, but by comparing entire supply chains. Even if labour costs are a quarter of those in China to make a given product, the unreliability or unavailability of many components may make it uneconomic to make things elsewhere.

Dwight Nordstrom of Pacific Resources International, a manufacturing consultancy, reckons China's supply chain for electronics manufacturers is so good that "there is no stopping the juggernaut" for at least ten to 20 years. This same advantage applies to low-tech industries, too. Paul Stocker of Topline, a shoe exporter with dozens of contract plants in coastal China, says there is no easy alternative to China.

It is fashionable to predict that China's inland factories will supplant its coastal ones. Official figures for foreign direct investment support this view: some inland provinces, such as Chongqing, now attract almost as much foreign money as Shanghai. The reason why fewer migrant workers from the hinterland are returning to coastal factories this year is that there are plenty of jobs closer to home.

The firms investing in China's interior are chiefly doing so to serve consumers who live there.

But manufacturers are not simply shifting inland in search of cheap labour. For one thing, it is not much cheaper. Huawei, a large Chinese telecoms firm, reports that salaries for engineers with a master's degree are not even 10% lower in its inland locations than in Shenzhen. Kolcraft considered shifting to Hubei, but found that total costs would end up being only 5–10% lower than on the coast.

Topline looked into moving inland, but found huge extra costs there. Infrastructure for exports is still shoddy or slow (shipping by river adds a week), logistics are not fully developed and Topline's entire supply chain remains on the coast. It decided to stay put.

Inland Revenue?

Moving inland brings all sorts of unexpected costs. Newish labour laws in wealthy places such as Shenzhen make it costlier to shut down plants there, for example. It can cost more to ship goods from the Chinese interior to the coast than from Shanghai to New York. Managers and other highly skilled staff often demand steep pay rises to move from sophisticated coastal cities to the boondocks. Chongqing has more than 30m [million] people, but it's not Shanghai. A recent anti-corruption campaign there grew so violent that it terrified legitimate businessfolk as well as crooks.

The firms investing in China's interior are chiefly doing so to serve consumers who live there. With so many inland cities booming, this is an enticing market. But when it comes to making iPads and smartphones for export, the world's workshop will remain in China's coastal provinces.

In time, of course, other places will build better roads and ports and supply chains. Eventually, they will challenge coastal China's grip on basic manufacturing. So if China is to flourish, its manufacturers must move up the value chain. Rather than bolting together sophisticated products designed elsewhere, they need to do more design work themselves. Taking a leaf out of Germany's book, they need to make products with higher margins and offer services to complement them.

Innovation and Chinese Manufacturing

A few Chinese firms have started to do this already. A visit to Huawei's huge corporate campus in Shenzhen is instructive. The firm was founded by a former military officer and has been helped by friends in government over the years, but it now more closely resembles a Western high-tech firm than it does a state-backed behemoth. Its managers are top-flight. Its leaders have for several years been learning from dozens of resident advisers from IBM and other American consultancies. It has become highly professional, and impressively innovative.

In 2008 it filed for more international patents than any other firm. Earlier this year, it unveiled the world's thinnest and fastest smartphones. In a sign that at least China's private sector is beginning to take intellectual-property rights seriously, Huawei is locked in bitter battles over patents, not only with multinationals but also with ZTE, a cross-town rival that also wants to shift from being a low-cost telecoms-equipment maker to a creator of sexy new consumer products.

China does not yet have enough Huaweis. But it attracts plenty of bright young people who would like to build one. Every year another wave of "sea turtles"—Chinese who have studied or worked abroad—returns home. Many have mixed with the world's best engineers at MIT and Stanford. Many have seen first-hand how Silicon Valley works. Indeed, Silicon Valley veterans have founded many of China's most innovative firms, such as Baidu.

The pace of change in China has been so startling that it is hard to keep up. The old stereotypes about low-wage sweatshops are as out-of-date as Mao suits. The next phase will be interesting: China must innovate or slow down.

6

China Is Not the Biggest Threat to American Manufacturing

Roger Pol

Roger Pol is a lifelong entrepreneur and the founder of the World Distance Learning Institute.

While many commentators have worried that competition from Chinese manufacturers is killing US manufacturing jobs, the truth is that the source of the problem is not Chinese competition but excessive regulation in the United States. Once, the United States allowed innovators the freedom to start and operate a business without a prohibitive amount of bureaucratic red tape. Today, however, many entrepreneurs are choosing to relocate to China to avoid the burdensome regulations in the country—making government oversight, not foreign competition, the biggest threat to US manufacturing.

One of the greatest threats facing our country today doesn't come from outside our borders. It's not the possibility of a terrorist attack. It is not the continually increasing illegal immigration across our southern border. It's not even the likelihood of a disrupted oil supply.

The greatest problem we face is the self-imposed cost and regulatory burden placed on the development of manufacturing businesses. America, at least the America I grew up in, was the land of the free and the home of the innovator. We used to celebrate entrepreneurs and reward those willing to take a risk. America, the "can do" America of my early years, allowed it's innovators to operate with relatively little restraint or restriction. If you wanted to start and operate a business, "have at it, we wish you success" was the motto of our great nation. If you had an idea for a "better mouse trap" build your plant, install your equipment, hire your people and good luck.

Have a great idea? See a viable opportunity? Want to build a product or establish a manufacturing plant? Go see your local government officials.

In the '60s we had a positive balance of trade and it was growing faster than anywhere else in the world. Japan, the second most industrialized country, produced goods that were considered inferior to those produced by our great American factories. China, South Korea, Mexico? Not even on the map! Today our balance of trade is negative by a long shot and the quality of our manufactured goods is inferior to that of many other countries. Much of what we consider manufacturing in the U.S. today is really the assembly of components manufactured in other countries. Manufacturing profits go to businesses outside America because we regulate manufacturing facilities into oblivion.

Bureaucratic Hurdles

Today the environment for starting and operating a manufacturing plant is not good. Gone are the days of "Great, go to it, do the best you can." Replaced by, "NIMBY"—Not In My Back Yard. The government has imposed itself as our costly overseer, placing environmental, zoning, and wage/benefit restrictions so burdensome in time and cost that businesses are left barely competitive if not impossible to begin.

Have a great idea? See a viable opportunity? Want to build a product or establish a manufacturing plant? Go see your local government officials. You will find the "go for it" attitude replaced with, Manufacturing??? Why do you want to consider such a dirty business? Why would you want to put your fellow citizens at risk? What would we do if someone were to get hurt? How could we possibly live with ourselves if, God forbid, some kind of particle escaped into the air or blew into a river? How could you live with yourself if your employees weren't all being treated equally and being supplied with incredibly attractive wages and benefits?

I would like to relate my recent experience trying to start a Carbon Fibre manufacturing company in a Northeastern U.S. State. After meeting for three weeks with the economic development offices of the State and City, it was determined that after I located and acquired a facility, at my cost and risk, even if it were properly zoned, it would have to be approved for a special use exception. Thereafter we were told to budget in excess of $300K [thousand] for pre-approval EPA [Environmental Protection Agency], environmental, and other studies. The studies would take about 6 months at minimum—with no guarantee of a successful outcome. Even if we were approved, and in spite of the fact that at opening we would be hiring approximately 25 technically competent people in a high unemployment region, we would have to go to the Union hall and negotiate a trades contract before hiring the first employee. I would be forced to unionize and hire more expensive, "senior union members." I am not allowed to go to Craigslist and hire younger, entry level trainees. My cost of operation becomes higher before even opening my doors and I have no choice in this matter. Unbelievable!!!

Even if I am willing to take the time, spend the money, and successfully navigate the bureaucratic hurdles, what additional risks do I face? How about this: OSHA [Occupational Safety and Health Administration] arbitrarily decides I'm not in compliance with one clause in their multi-thousand page regulatory bible. Or, an employee-union member decides he is not being treated fairly or that the benefits package is not equal to that of federal or state employees, and files a grievance. How about the EPA deciding, retroactively, that in the event of a power outage there is a chance my factory might leak a "toxic" substance? I will be sued, shut down and possibly prosecuted criminally.

Setting Up Shop in China

Now, consider my experience the last time I visited China. I was escorted by the governor of Tianjin State to one of his new cities and shown the process to open a manufacturing facility. I was led into a room with a series of desks. You start at the first desk where you present your plan. Thereafter you proceed from one to the next obtaining approvals or agree to modifications on the spot until at the last table where you are shown what lots and buildings are available that best suit your needs and the price of each. The total timeline for permits, from beginning to approval, takes about 3 hours.

The greatest threat to our American future doesn't come from other nations, it comes from within.

At the end of the line you pay your fee, get your permit, and choose your construction manager if a new building is necessary. The city designates the building team to come the following day and begin construction. Generally you are guaranteed that you will be able to move your equipment in within 5 months.

There are no restrictions on importation of equipment, state officials help with marketing and sales inside the country and do not restrict exportation of the manufactured goods or profits. Now, this is China so the government and the state share 30% of your business, but considering the ease of entry, increased in-country sales and helpful attitude, this is a small price to pay, especially considering America's 35% plus corporate tax rates. Also, if the price of the lot or building seems high, and they like your project, they will negotiate the price and terms.

This is why our balance of trade is so out of whack. This is why many companies move out of the United States for foreign environs. This is why the United States is losing its position as the greatest manufacturing country in the world.

The greatest threat to our American future doesn't come from other nations, it comes from within. We have become our own worst enemy.

7

US Manufacturers Will Return Stateside as Wages Rise in China

David Conrads

David Conrads is a contributor to the Christian Science Monitor.

Beginning in the 1990s, many US manufactures began "offshoring," paying low-wage workers in China to make their products. Today, however, many of these firms are moving back for a variety of reasons, including the rising cost of labor in China, quality issues, and difficulty with oversight when the production plant is thousands of miles away. While all manufacturing has not returned to the United States, this general trend will add needed jobs to the US economy.

A & E Custom Manufacturing hums with the sound of robotic presses and welders, automated laser cutters, and other state-of the-art equipment that bend and cut metal into precise shapes. More than 900 sheet-metal components for the New York City subway come from this shop, as do aluminum parts for an electric sports car in Finland.

The Kansas City, Kan., metal fabricator also made parts for a popular commercial cooking appliance until several years ago, when its customer moved production to China in order to save money. When quality and delivery problems in

China couldn't be resolved, the customer brought the work back and A & E is once again making the parts.

"We're doing the work we used to do," says A & E owner Steve Hasty. "We've become more competitive in what we're doing and the type of equipment that we're using."

Returning to the US

Call it reshoring, backshoring, or onshoring: Twenty years after a flood of American manufacturers began moving to China to cut costs, a growing number of them are trickling back to the United States to improve quality and reduce delays. Many of the high labor-content products, like shoes, textiles and most clothing are probably gone forever. But in an unexpected and beneficial twist for the US economy, manufacturing, much of it high-skilled, is returning from abroad, primarily China. Some analysts go so far as to call it a renaissance in US manufacturing that will create high-paying jobs and provide crucial economic support for local communities across the country.

"A combination of economic forces is fast eroding China's cost advantage as an export platform for the North American market," says Boston Consulting Group [BCG] in a report issued last summer, which forecast that by sometime around 2015 it will be as economical to manufacture many goods for US consumption in the US as in China. BCG points to seven industries that are nearing that break-even point: electronics, appliances, machinery, transportation goods, fabricated metals, furniture, and plastics and rubber—all products with relatively low labor content and high transportation costs.

Some US companies have already made the move:

- Two years ago, General Electric relocated the production of some water heaters from China to Louisville, Ky.

- NCR has moved production of its automated teller machines from China to a plant in Columbus, Ga., that's expected to employ 870 people by 2014.

- Ford Motor Co. is bringing up to 2,000 jobs back to the US from Mexico, China, and Japan.

- Even toy company Wham-O now manufactures half of its popular Frisbees in California and Michigan, where it previously sourced its goods from China and Mexico.

How many jobs reshoring is creating is hard to determine. When a large, well-known company like Master Lock brings 100 jobs from China to its factory in Milwaukee—and earns a visit from President Obama and a mention in his State of the Union address—it's big news. When a small contract manufacturer gets an order for components previously made offshore, it's barely noticed.

US manufactures have also made strides through "lean" manufacturing techniques and automation.

"It's definitely happening," says Harry Moser, founder of the Reshoring Initiative, a nonprofit organization based in greater Chicago whose goal is to bring manufacturing jobs back to the US. "It's still small relative to its potential, but it's growing." He estimates reshoring has created at least 10,000 American jobs in the past two years.

Production Costs and Labor

One big factor behind the move is the rising cost of labor in China. When it joined the World Trade Organization in 2001, China's average manufacturing wage was 58 cents an hour, says Harold Sirkin, senior partner at the Chicago office of BCG and one of the coauthors of its report. Since then, Chinese wages have risen 15 to 20 percent per year.

"The decisions you made when wages were 58 cents an hour are potentially going to look very different than when wages are around $6 per hour, as they will be in China in

2015," Mr. Sirkin says. When the cost savings of manufacturing offshore is less than 10 percent of manufacturing domestically, companies start to reassess their decisions, he adds.

US manufacturers have also made strides through "lean" manufacturing techniques and automation, which have made factories far less labor-intensive than in the past, says Chris Kuehl, an independent economist in Kansas City, Mo., and an analyst for the Fabricators & Manufacturers Association, a trade group in Rockford, Ill. BCG estimates that the average US worker is now some 3.4 times more productive than the average Chinese worker. "That takes us out of having to compete with China for low-wage jobs, because we're producing things that require more sophisticated robotics," Mr. Kuehl adds.

Other considerations also factor into reshoring decisions: transportation costs, proximity to customers, currency fluctuations, the benefits to innovation when design and production are under the same roof, and intellectual property risk, among others.

If today's reshoring trickle turns into something much bigger, the benefits to the US economy look promising— and not just for manufacturers.

For many companies, low wages overseas don't outweigh the advantage of making goods closer to the customer. Outdoor GreatRoom Co., maker of outdoor products, brought production of fire pits and pergolas back to Minnesota in 2010 to reduce the several-month lag time in getting shipments from China. Now, the company can fill its orders in three months or less, which reduces the risk that the company is locked in to an older inventory that no longer corresponds with consumer tastes.

In the case of Big W Industries, which brought back the work to A & E for its commercial cooking appliance, the issue was quality.

"We went overseas to try to cut costs," says Chuck Nickloy, president of the Kansas City, Kan., firm. "We brought things back because of quality. We tried a couple of times to get the job done right, but the thousands of units we brought in were all substandard. Before it was over, we scrapped them all. It was a nightmare."

The Future of US Manufacturing

Not all the manufacturing moving from China is coming back to the US. Some of it is going to lower-cost countries in Asia, like Vietnam and Singapore. Many US companies are likely to keep some production in China because they want to sell into its fast-growing domestic market. Other US firms are opting for "near-shoring," moving manufacturing from Asia to Mexico or Central America, where they can take advantage of low wages but reduce transportation costs and other problems that go with having a supply chain that stretches halfway around the world.

Reshoring or even near-shoring may not work for everyone, cautions Mr. Sirkin, who consults with many manufacturing firms. "That may not be the right answer for you in the same way that rushing to China or Vietnam may not be the right answer."

But if today's reshoring trickle turns into something much bigger, the benefits to the US economy look promising—and not just for manufacturers. By one estimate, each new domestic manufacturing job creates three additional jobs in the US, in logistics, transportation, construction, finance, and other areas. With a renewed focus on technical education, far from becoming a nation of hamburger flippers, the US could be poised to reclaim at least some of the 7.7 million manufacturing jobs it has lost since 1979.

8

The US Trade Deficit with China Has Cost American Jobs

Robert E. Scott

Robert E. Scott is the director of trade and manufacturing research at the Economic Policy Institute.

The trade imbalance between China and the United States has led to nearly three million job losses in America. While the biggest impact has been in the computer and electronic industries, the trade deficit has impacted numerous industries and the workforce of every US state. With a growing trade deficit favoring China, the United States will continue to lose more jobs than it gains in this relationship. Only a fundamental change in the trade agreements between the two countries can help resolve this imbalance.

Since China entered the World Trade Organization [WTO] in 2001, the extraordinary growth of U.S. trade with China has had a dramatic effect on U.S. workers and the domestic economy. The United States is piling up foreign debt and losing export capacity, and the growing trade deficit with China has been a prime contributor to the crisis in U.S. manufacturing employment. Between 2001 and 2010, the trade deficit with China eliminated or displaced 2.8 million jobs, 1.9 mil-

Robert E. Scott, "Growing U.S. Trade Deficit with China Cost 2.8 Million Jobs Between 2001 and 2010: Hundreds to thousands of jobs displaced in every U.S. congressional district," *Economic Policy Institute*, Vol. 323, September 20, 2011, pp. 1–3, 8, 18. Copyright © 2011 by Economic Policy Institute. All rights reserved. Reproduced by permission.

lion (69.2 percent) of which were in manufacturing. The 1.9 million manufacturing jobs eliminated or displaced due to trade with China represents *nearly half* of all U.S. manufacturing jobs lost or displaced between China's entry into WTO and 2010.

The 2.8 million jobs lost or displaced in all sectors include 453,100 jobs lost or displaced from 2008 to 2010 alone—even though imports from China and the rest of world collapsed in 2009. (Imports from China have since recovered and surpassed their peak in 2008.) The growing trade deficit with China has cost jobs in every congressional district, including the District of Columbia and Puerto Rico.

The trade deficit in the computer and electronic parts industry grew the most, displacing 909,400 jobs—32.6% of all jobs displaced between 2001 and 2010. As a result, the hardest-hit congressional districts were in California, Texas, Oregon, and Massachusetts, where remaining jobs in those industries are concentrated. Some districts in North Carolina, Georgia, and Colorado were also especially hard hit by job displacement in a variety of manufacturing industries, including computers and electronic parts, textiles and apparel, and furniture.

Most of the jobs lost or displaced by trade with China between 2001 and 2010 were in manufacturing industries.

But the jobs impact of the China trade deficit is not restricted to job loss and displacement. Competition with low-wage workers from less-developed countries such as China has driven down wages for workers in U.S. manufacturing and reduced the wages and bargaining power of similar, non-college educated workers throughout the economy. The affected population includes essentially all workers with less than a four-year college degree—roughly 70% of the workforce (2009), or about 100 million workers.

Put another way, for a typical full-time median-wage earner in 2006, earnings losses due to globalization totaled approximately $1,400. China is the most important source of downward wage pressure from trade with less-developed countries, because it pays very low wages and because its products make up such a large portion of U.S. imports (China was responsible for 54% of U.S. non-oil imports from less-developed countries in 2010).

These conclusions about the jobs impact of trade with China arise from the following specific findings of this study:

- Most of the jobs lost or displaced by trade with China between 2001 and 2010 were in manufacturing industries (1.93 million jobs, or 69.2%).

- Within manufacturing, rapidly growing imports of computer and electronic parts (including computers, parts, semiconductors, and audio-video equipment) accounted for more than 44% of the $194 billion increase in the U.S. trade deficit with China between 2001 and 2010. The growth of this deficit contributed to the elimination of 909,400 U.S. jobs in computer and electronic products in this period. Indeed, in 2010, the total U.S. trade deficit with China was $278.3 billion—$124.3 billion of which was in computer and electronic parts.

- Global trade in advanced technology products [ATP]—often discussed as a source of comparative advantage for the United States—is instead dominated by China. This broad category of high-end technology products includes the more advanced elements of the computer and electronic parts industry as well as other sectors such as biotechnology, life sciences, aerospace, and nuclear technology. In 2010, the United States had a $94.2 billion deficit in advanced technology products with China, which was responsible for 34% of the total U.S.-China trade deficit. In contrast, the United States had a $13.3 billion surplus in ATP with the rest of the world in 2010.

- Other industrial sectors hit hard by growing trade deficits with China between 2001 and 2010 include apparel and accessories (178,700 jobs), textile fabrics and products (92,300), fabricated metal products (123,900), plastic and rubber products (62,000), motor vehicles and parts (49,300), and miscellaneous manufactured goods (119,700). Several service sectors were also hit hard by indirect job losses including administrative, support, and waste management services (204,300) and professional, scientific, and technical services (173,100).

- The 2.8 million U.S. jobs lost or displaced by the trade deficit with China between 2001 and 2010 were distributed among all 50 states, the District of Columbia, and Puerto Rico, with the biggest net losses occurring in California (454,600 jobs), Texas (232,800), New York (161,400), Illinois (118,200), Florida (114,400), North Carolina (107,800), Pennsylvania (106,900), Ohio (103,500), Massachusetts (88,600), and Georgia (87,700).

- Jobs displaced due to growing deficits with China exceeded 2.2% of total employment in the 10 hardest-hit states (i.e., jobs lost or displaced as a share of total state employment): New Hampshire (19,700, 2.84%), California (454,600, 2.74%), Massachusetts (88,600, 2.73%), Oregon (47,900, 2.71%), North Carolina (107,800, 2.61%) Minnesota (70,700, 2.61%), Idaho (17,400, 2.54%), Vermont (7,800 2.37%), Colorado (55,800, 2.30%), and Rhode Island (11,800, 2.24%).

- The hardest-hit congressional districts were concentrated in states that were heavily exposed to growing China trade deficits in computer and electronic products and other industries such as furniture, textiles, apparel, and durable goods manufacturing. The three hardest-hit Congressional districts were all located in Silicon Valley in California, including the 15th (Santa Clara County, 39,669 jobs, 12.23% of all jobs in the district), the 14th (Palo Alto and nearby cities, 28,866 jobs, 9.0%), and the 16th (San Jose and other parts of Santa Clara County, 26,478 jobs, 8.72%). Of the top 20 hardest-hit districts, eight were in California (in rank order, the 15th, 14th, 16th, 13th, 31st, 34th, 50th, and 47th), four were in Texas (31st, 10th, 25th, and 3rd), three were in North Carolina (4th, 10th and 6th), two were in Massachusetts (5th and 3rd), and one each in Oregon (1st), Georgia (9th), and Colorado (4th). Each of these districts lost at least 9,500 jobs or 3.4% of its total jobs. One-fourth of the hardest-hit 20 districts (representing about 1% of the nation's 435 congressional districts) lost at least 20,000 jobs apiece or 5.8% percent of their total jobs.

The job displacement estimates in this study are conservative. They include only the direct and indirect jobs displaced by trade, and exclude jobs in domestic wholesale and retail trade and advertising. The U.S. unemployment rate averaged 9.6 percent in 2010. During the Great Recession of 2007–2009, and continuing through 2010, jobs displaced by China trade reduced wages and spending, which led to further job losses in the economy. This spillover effect certainly arose from the loss of 453,100 jobs due to growing trade deficits with China between 2008 and 2010. . . .

Growing Trade Deficits and Job Losses

Each $1 billion in exports to China from the United States supports American jobs. However, each $1 billion in imports from China displaces the American workers who would have been employed making these products in the United States. On balance, the net employment effect of trade depends on the changes in the trade balance. An improving trade balance can support job creation, but growing trade deficits usually result in growing net U.S. job displacement. The United States has had large trade deficits with China since 2001, which increased in every year except 2009, when U.S. trade with all countries collapsed due to the recession of 2007–2009.

The employment impacts of the growing U.S. trade deficit with China are estimated in this paper using an input-output model that estimates the direct and indirect labor requirements of producing output in a given domestic industry. The model includes 202 U.S. industries, 84 of which are in the manufacturing sector....

On average, 310,000 jobs per year have been lost or displaced since China's entry into the WTO.

The model estimates the amount of labor (number of jobs) required to produce a given volume of exports and the labor displaced when a given volume of imports is substituted for domestic output. The difference between these two numbers is essentially the jobs displaced by growing trade deficits, holding all else equal.

Jobs displaced by the growing China trade deficit are a net drain on employment in trade-related industries, especially those in manufacturing. Even if increases in demand in other sectors absorb all the workers displaced by trade (an unlikely event), job quality will likely suffer because many non-traded industries such as retail trade and home health care pay lower wages and have less comprehensive benefits than traded-goods industries.

U.S. exports to China in 2001 supported 168,900 jobs, but U.S. imports displaced production that would have supported 1,071,500 jobs. Therefore, the $84 billion trade deficit in 2001 displaced 902,600 jobs in that year. Job displacement rose to 3,239,600 jobs in 2008 and 3,692,700 jobs in 2010.

Since China's entry into the WTO in 2001 and through 2010, the increase in U.S.-China trade deficits eliminated or displaced 2,790,100 U.S. jobs. Between 2008 and 2010 alone 453,100 jobs were lost, either by the elimination of existing jobs or by the prevention of new job creation. On average, 310,000 jobs per year have been lost or displaced since China's entry into the WTO. The continuing growth in job displacement between 2008 and 2010 despite the relatively small increase in the trade deficit reflects the relatively rapid growth of U.S. imports of computer and electronics products from China, and the fact that the price index for most of these products fell continuously throughout the study period, as noted below. The share of computer and electronic parts in U.S. imports from China (in current, nominal dollars) increased from 32.9% in 2008 to 37.3% in 2010 alone. . . .

The Need for Fundamental Change

The growing U.S. trade deficit with China has displaced millions of jobs in the United States and contributed heavily to the crisis in U.S. manufacturing employment, which has heightened over the last decade largely due to trade with China. Moreover, the United States is piling up foreign debt, losing export capacity, and facing a more fragile macroeconomic environment.

Is America's loss China's gain? The answer is not clearly affirmative. China has become dependent on the U.S. consumer market for employment generation, suppressed the purchasing power of its own middle class with a weak currency, and, most important, now holds over $3 trillion in hard currency reserves instead of investing them in public goods that could benefit Chinese households. Its vast purchases of foreign exchange reserves have stimulated the overheating of its domestic economy, and inflation in China has accelerated rapidly in the past year. Its repression of labor rights has suppressed wages, thereby artificially subsidizing exports.

The U.S-China trade relationship needs a fundamental change. Addressing the exchange rate policies and labor standards issues in the Chinese economy are important first steps.

9

The US and China's Economic Rivalry Creates International Tensions

Ian Bremmer

Ian Bremmer is a political scientist and blogger whose writing has been published in the Washington Post *and the* New York Times, *as well as other publications.*

The rise of China as an economic powerhouse offers a challenge to US dominance. Earlier, when China began to grow, the country worked with the United States to resolve trade conflicts. Increasingly, however, China has been willing to "go its own way." Both politically and economically, China has resisted democratic and market reforms, preferring state-controlled capitalism. In the process, the Chinese economic miracle has raised standards for many within the country. On the world market, however, there have been—and remain—a number of obstacles. China, for example, frequently ignores intellectual property rights, creating tensions with American companies (like Google). Unfortunately, many of these clashes will only grow worse over time. While it seems unlikely that these differences will lead to military conflict, even that cannot be ruled out over the longterm.

At the World Economic Forum in Davos [Switzerland] this January [2010], Chinese vice premier, Li Keqiang, gave an entirely unremarkable speech. Steering clear of subjects that make headlines, he instead sung the praises of China's stability and technological progress. Yet the moment was made extraordinary by Li's entourage: a group of about 75 subordinates who laughed, cheered and applauded on cue—and all with apparently genuine gusto. This scene brought to my mind Deng Xiaoping's famous dictum that his country must "keep a low profile and never take the lead." There was plenty of Chinese exuberance in the room, and the rest of us were meant to notice. Has the need to lie low subsided, I wondered? Does China believe that its time has come?

That was the message many people took from the triumphalist pageantry of Beijing's 2008 Olympics. But the real game-changer was economic. The financial crisis, global recession, and China's remarkable recovery have produced a big shift in the world's most important state-to-state relationship. Chinese officials argue that their country's resilience in the face of America's meltdown has vindicated a Chinese model of development, one that rejects US-style free markets in favour of a "state capitalist" system. A relationship until recently shaped mainly by shared interests must now adapt to accommodate the two sides' increasingly divergent views of capitalism—and a large shift in the balance of confidence.

We will see more public Chinese pushback against what Beijing considers "interference" from Washington in months to come.

The list of irritants in US-Chinese relations is growing. Google threatens to quit China over censorship and cyber-attacks. Washington and Beijing are at cross purposes over Iran's nuclear programme. US lawmakers have again criticised China's unwillingness to allow the value of its currency to rise and its failure to protect the intellectual property of foreign companies. There are trade disputes over tyres [tires] and steel pipes. Yet these problems are merely symptoms of an illness that has progressed further than some observers realise.

Put bluntly, the Chinese leadership no longer believes that American power is as indispensable as it once was for either China's economic expansion or the Communist party's political survival. Nor does it accept that access to US capital or commercial know-how is quite so important for the next stage of China's development—or that its growth depends on the spending habits of American consumers.

Economic "Decoupling"

China has embarked on a process of economic "decoupling." The western financial meltdown put millions of Chinese out of work in early 2009, as factories that produced goods for export closed their doors. Over the past 18 months, Beijing has seen how dependence on western markets can produce unacceptably high levels of risk at home. The solution is to shift its model to rely more on China's growing consumer base. This plan, however, must be undertaken with great care to ensure minimum industrial disruption.

Meanwhile, China's political decoupling from the west is also in full swing. We saw it at December's climate change summit in Copenhagen, as China spearheaded resistance from developing states to western-proposed targets on carbon emissions. We saw it in the strong reaction to an announcement in February of US arms sales to Taiwan and to Barack Obama's meeting with the Dalai Lama days later. We will see more public Chinese pushback against what Beijing considers "interference" from Washington in months to come.

There is still considerable mutual dependence between the US and China, grounded mainly in commercial ties. But the unfolding conflict is in many ways more dangerous than the cold war. Economic decision-making in Moscow had little impact on western power or standards of living. But globalisation means there is no equivalent to the Berlin wall, insulating China and America from turmoil inside the other.

The rivalry may take on a life of its own, growing beyond the governments' ability to contain it. American policymakers must ensure that US power remains indispensable to China's rise. This will not be a popular undertaking in Washington. Facing voters this November [2010], US politicians will want to shift the blame for the country's woes onto someone else. Cultural conservatives of the right and labour champions of the left will tell voters that their problems are made in China. Even more sober figures are beginning to raise the alarm, as when economist Paul Krugman warned in March 2010 that China's economic policy "seriously damages the rest of the world."

Building China's economy meant establishing the country as an export powerhouse.

Soon, more Americans will be asking why a country with 10 per cent unemployment can't persuade a country with 10 per cent growth to respect trade rules and play a responsible role on the global stage. And Beijing's new assertiveness is feeding a growing insecurity in the US. In a survey conducted by the Pew Research Centre in 2009, 44 per cent of Americans named China as "the world's leading economic power." Just 27 per cent chose the US. Reasonable or not, this is a sea change in attitudes—2008 was the last presidential election in which average voters didn't know or care where the candidates stood on China.

Building the Chinese Economy

How did we get here? For the past 30 years, China's rise and America's power have been complementary. In the late 1970s, the Chinese leadership began to tinker with capitalism and to cautiously open the country to foreign trade and investment.

Less hawkish officials in Washington and Beijing hoped that a relationship could be built, but fallout from the Tiananmen Square massacre in 1989 put their plans on hold. As the Warsaw pact governments fell later that year and the Soviet empire followed in 1991, China's hardliners applied the brakes on capitalist experimentation. But in 1992, 88-year-old Deng Xiaoping breathed new life into market reform. Deng's successor, Jiang Zemin, beat back old guard resistance to liberalisation, and stepped up the pace of reform in the early 1990s.

The collapse of European communism taught China's leadership that to hold onto power, it must succeed where other socialist states had failed by offering people a rising standard of living. Building China's economy meant establishing the country as an export powerhouse, a plan that required access to consumers in the US, EU [European Union] and Japan— still China's three largest trading partners. That meant opening the economy to ever-higher levels of foreign trade and investment—effectively "coupling" China's growth to the west's.

US companies were happy to oblige. Wal-Mart became the world's largest retailer because its founder, Sam Walton, recognised the possibilities of low-cost Chinese labour. In the years since, a growing number of American companies have begun banking on huge profits based on sales to China's potentially enormous middle class. In turn, Chinese companies looking to move up the value chain have benefited from exposure to the management, advanced technologies and marketing techniques of US, European and Japanese companies.

Beijing's relationship with the US reached a crucial moment in January 1993, when Bill Clinton entered the White House. As a candidate Clinton had denounced China's leaders as "butchers," and promised to end the "most favoured nation" trade status that China had enjoyed since 1980. As president, Clinton proved more circumspect, pursuing a policy of "constructive engagement." US consumers benefited as cheap Chinese products helped to keep inflation in check during the

1990s. Before leaving office, Clinton signed into law "permanent normal trade relations" between the two countries. The relationship had become too big to fail.

The Communist party is using markets to create wealth that can be directed as officials see fit.

At the time, Beijing had good reason to value American power and Washington's willingness to use it. Developing trade and investment relationships with potentially volatile emerging states in Africa, the middle east, southeast Asia and Latin America exposed China to risks it had little experience in managing. America's willingness to play the global policeman helped open and maintain trade routes and sea lanes for Chinese companies. Expanded access to US consumers helped China's economy create millions of jobs. Washington proved willing (for the most part) to respect Chinese sensitivities on Taiwan, Tibet and Tiananmen Square.

In 2001, China joined the World Trade Organisation: a landmark moment in its embrace of the global status quo. In the years since, the creative destruction that comes with decades of double-digit growth has created big problems inside China: the disparities of wealth between coastal cities and the rest of the country, serious environmental damage and social unrest. To ensure a more "harmonious" rise, a new generation of leaders led by President Hu Jintao and Premier Wen Jiabao has taken a direct hand in managing expansion. The government already relied heavily on state-owned companies to secure access to resources. It now began to use privately owned companies to dominate certain sectors: Yingli and Suntech have taken over the solar-power industry; BYD dominates batteries and cars. Beijing relies on both public and private sectors to manage the pace of growth and the distribution of its benefits. And sovereign wealth funds, created from the country's enormous reserves of foreign currency—the People's

Bank of China valued the country's holdings at $2.399 trillion (£1.580 trillion) in December 2009—are used to direct huge flows of investment.

In sum, the Communist party is using markets to create wealth that can be directed as officials see fit. The ultimate motive is not economic but political: to maximise the state's control of development and the leadership's chance of survival. It is a model that has so far been strikingly successful—to the extent that China no longer needs to keep a low profile and let the US take the lead. But it is not a system that offers a level-playing field to foreign companies and investors.

Growing Pains

The signs of decoupling are all around us. In January, Google claimed that its proprietary source code and the Gmail accounts of human rights activists had been targeted in a sophisticated cyber-attack from inside China. In response, the company threatened to quit the Chinese market. It remains unclear whether the Chinese government played a direct role in the attacks, condones them, or is simply unable to stop them. The government promotes "indigenous innovation," a vaguely articulated plan to encourage homegrown intellectual property and the companies that develop it. Some of that innovation has been stolen. Google's charges placed the issue of Chinese cyber-espionage in the headlines, but the problem has been building for years. Following the Gulf war in 1991, the Chinese government saw the need to invest in the information warfare capabilities of the People's Liberation Army. At first, cyber-espionage was mainly confined to the military realm, but in the past three years it seems to have expanded into the corporate world.

Beyond the espionage problem, China's ambitions have provoked a sharp response from high-tech companies in the US and Europe. They charge that China's policy of favouring products made with domestically created intellectual property proves that Beijing is no longer even pretending to observe international intellectual property rules. That's why the Google story is not really about censorship or state persecution of dissidents. It is mainly about Baidu, Google's main Chinese rival. Baidu already holds the dominant market share within China, and if Google leaves or is forced out, Baidu will benefit the most. Companies such as Baidu have growing influence within China's state bureaucracy and have also become symbols of pride for the government and public.

In January [2010], the US government announced a plan to sell $6.4bn [billion] in weaponry to Taiwan. This kind of deal was sure to provoke an angry response from the mainland, and it did. But this time Beijing added an extraordinary threat: the imposition of sanctions on US aircraft manufacturer Boeing, which dominates China's airline market, worth $400bn over the next 20 years. Were Boeing to lose this business, some of it would surely fall to European aircraft-maker Airbus. But over time, more of it would move to emerging Chinese companies.

The predicaments of Boeing and Google illustrate how the US and Chinese brands of capitalism are pushing Washington and Beijing towards conflict. For the moment, the governments' incentives for co-operation outweigh any advantage that either can find in direct confrontation. But the forces that divide them are too large for either side to fully control.

There is also trouble looming over the dollar. As China moves to shift from exports to greater domestic consumption, the need to purchase dollars will lessen and much of the extra cash will flow into the purchase of commodities. America will then have to look elsewhere to make up the difference in financing its debt. This larger shift in the balance of power in the relationship will also empower Chinese hawks to call for greater resistance to US pressure on places like Iran, Burma and Sudan. Chinese state-owned companies have established lucrative commercial relationships with these governments—

ties that serve China's interests. In exchange, China provides these governments with the resources and political cover they need to reject US and European demands for policy change.

China will not mount a military challenge to the US any time soon.

Chinese and US Tensions

Back at Davos, tensions were evident during an exchange between Zhu Min, the deputy governor of the People's Bank of China, and the Democratic congressman Barney Frank of Massachusetts. Zhu was questioned on China's currency. "It is very important to have a stable yuan. . . . It is good for China and good for the world," Zhu said. "Could it be stable but a little higher?" Frank asked. The audience laughed. Zhu smiled, unperturbed. No need to explain your strategy when you're holding a winning hand. Nonetheless, the same dispute broke into the open again in March 2010, when Premier Wen Jiabao slapped down calls by another group of American lawmakers for China to allow its currency to appreciate.

Last autumn, Washington moved against Chinese exports of tyres and steel pipes to protect American companies and jobs in these industries. But the next conflict will extend well beyond trade. In December [2009], Senate Majority Leader Harry Reid sent an open letter to President Hu Jintao in which he accused China of, among other things, pursuing "a policy to undermine American competitiveness . . . while simultaneously benefiting from open access to the US market" and "rampant intellectual property theft." There is an abundance of bootleg Windows software in China, for example, something Microsoft has been unable to control; it's estimated that up to 80 per cent of all software sold in the country is pirated. When congress debates energy policy later this year, Republicans will demand to know why the US should accept binding commitments on carbon emissions that undermine its competitiveness while China refuses to follow suit. In turn, China's fast-growing blogosphere will ask why free market champions in the US are threatening them with protectionism.

China will not mount a military challenge to the US any time soon. Its economy and living standards have grown so quickly over the past two decades that it's hard to imagine the kind of catastrophic event that could push its leadership to risk it all. Beijing knows that no US government will support Taiwanese independence, and China need not invade an island that it has largely co-opted already by offering Taiwan's business elite privileged investment opportunities.

Today, the US and China are locked in a new form of "mutually assured economic destruction."

That said, China's determination to defend its territorial integrity, its ambitions to extend its influence in Asia, and its plan to form new commercial partnerships in far-flung places have given momentum to military plans. With 2.3m [million] soldiers under arms, the People's Liberation Army is already the world's largest. Its investments in cyberwarfare technology continue to cause anxiety in Washington. Its military budget is thought to have tripled between 2003 and 2009 to about $70bn. This is only 13 per cent of what the US spends each year, but significant enough to pose future challenges.

Any cold war-type conflict is much more likely to develop over issues of economic security than military confrontation. Charges of Chinese corporate espionage will complicate the efforts of Chinese companies to invest in the US. China will respond with investment restrictions of its own. And western companies will find themselves competing for natural resources across the developing world with Chinese state-owned companies, armed with subsidies and political backing. This is already happening openly in places like Nigeria and Ghana, and there is more subtle competition taking place from Angola to Venezuela to Iraq. China and other authoritarian governments that embrace state capitalism will increasingly direct trade flows toward one another, lowering the trajectory of economic growth in the west. Finally, though China's military will not offer the US a global challenge, it can certainly take on American forces in Asia.

Exploiting US Advantages

So how should America respond? The country's cold war experience offers a useful strategy. The stalemate imposed by "mutually assured destruction" that prevented the US-Soviet conflict from igniting created a sense of stability. Today, the US and China are locked in a new form of "mutually assured economic destruction," a dependence that can force some degree of cooperation even as political, economic and security disputes simmer. America still needs China to help finance its debt. For the moment, China needs access to US consumers to keep unemployment in check and for continuing foreign investment. Even if the Chinese economy becomes more driven by domestic demand, consumers will still want access to foreign-made products. The two sides will be doing business for decades to come.

US officials should do their best to ensure that this "mutually assured economic destruction" continues. But in Washington's poisonous political climate, populist opportunists will cast engagement as appeasement. With criticism of China from both left and right, those who see the wisdom of deepening mutual dependence will need courage—particularly when China's leaders criticise US policy to appease hardliners within the leadership, and a restive population.

American (and other foreign) companies doing business in China can take lessons from how multinational oil companies have adapted to a world in which state-owned energy companies control at least 80 per cent of the global oil reserves—by shifting their business models to exploit their remaining comparative advantages. To compete with state-owned energy operations, multinationals now invest in the project management and advanced technology that their rivals can't yet match. Foreign companies in China should similarly invest more heavily in products with a blazing-fast product cycle, like advanced electronics and videogaming. By the time their Chinese rivals have broken the code on this intellectual property, they will already have a newer model. And given the greying of China's population, foreign investment will remain welcome in healthcare innovations. There are many such examples.

Post-cold war US hegemony didn't last long. But there is no coherent alliance of rising powers to contain the American colossus.

It is also important for the US government and American companies to invest in those areas where their comparative advantage is most likely to endure. For Washington, that means maintaining US "hard power" advantages. Soft power helped America survive the cold war, and continues to play a crucial role in extending US influence. But over the next several years, hard power will ensure that the US remains indispensable for global political and economic stability.

The United States's Military Edge

The US now spends more on its military capacity than all potential competitors combined. It outspends China by about eight to one. Even if defence spending were significantly reduced, the US will hold a dominant military position for the foreseeable future, because it will be decades before any rival will prove both willing and able to accept the burdens that come with global leadership. China will continue to expand its influence, particularly within Asia. But it makes little sense for a still developing nation to challenge US hard power outside its immediate neighbourhood—particularly when China's state-owned oil companies will rely for several decades on oil and gas supplies from unstable parts of the world such as the middle east, the Caspian sea basin and west Africa. In addition, the presence of US troops in Japan and South Korea limits the risk of an Asian arms race. That saves China, Japan, South Korea and India a great deal of money.

Finally, America will have to get by with a little help from its friends. US relations with Japan have been tested over the past year as the Obama administration and the new Democratic party of Japan-led government re-establish the common interests that bind the two countries. The Clinton and George W Bush administrations built closer ties with India; that work should be broadened and deepened. The US should co-ordinate more closely with the EU—and its most influential member states—on ways to create a unified front in trade disputes with Beijing.

Post-cold war US hegemony didn't last long. But there is no coherent alliance of rising powers to contain the American colossus. Instead, the speed with which ideas, information, people, money, goods and services now cross borders has enabled a host of nations to make a mark on the international stage—just at a moment when the US is overstretched militarily, and its responses to international terrorism have exacerbated global anti-Americanism. And no single relationship will play a larger role in shaping Washington's response to the messy new order that is now emerging than its increasingly troubled relations with Beijing.

10

China's Growing Film Industry May Provide Competition for Hollywood

Ellen E. Jones

Ellen E. Jones is a film journalist based in the United Kingdom.

China is on its way to becoming the second largest film market, leading to increased competition with Hollywood. While Hollywood attempts to capture the partially untapped Chinese market, Chinese filmmakers work to win its domestic audience, as well as attract international filmgoers. And as American filmmakers struggle to offer a Hollywood version of China for domestic and foreign viewers, Chinese filmmakers struggle to represent themselves within the quickly expanding film industry in their country.

Po, the Kung Fu Panda, may look like an innocuous, chubby animal, but he could turn out to be the most devastating double agent on the world stage since Mata Hari shimmied her way to infamy in the first world war. Last week, the sequel to the Chinese-themed, US-made animation broke box-office records in China, taking 125m [million] yuan (#11m [pounds]) in its opening weekend. It's great news for its creators at DreamWorks, mildly irritating news for Chinese animators and intriguing news for the rest of the cinemagoing world, coming just as a newly confident China squares up to the original moviemaking superpower.

In Hollywood, movies that borrow far-eastern exoticism to entertain western audiences are as old as Mann's Chinese The-atre—and usually as authentically Chinese. Kung fu movies have been popular in the west since the 70s, and Hong Kong cinema gained its own foothold when director John Woo exported his signature "gun fu" to Hollywood with *The Killer* in 1989, following in person four years later.

What is new, however, is the tempting prospect of more than a billion *Avatar*-appreciating movie fans in mainland China. Already the world's second largest economy, China is set to overtake Japan and become the second largest cinema market after the US. According to the predictions of the China Film Producers' Association, by 2015 China will have built more than 7,000 new cinemas, and have annual box-office receipts of up to #3.7bn—which would explain Hollywood's increasingly unsubtle efforts to woo Chinese audiences. Last year's remake of *The Karate Kid* replaced Japanese karate with Chinese kung fu and a California setting for a Beijing location shoot. Seth Rogen's version of *The Green Hornet* passed over more obvious casting choices for the role of the sidekick Kato in favour of Jay Chou, who was little-known in the west, but a bankable heartthrob in the far east.

China's economic prosperity affords it the opportunity to present its own image to the world, unmediated by Hollywood.

Like a suitor spurned, in 2007 the US also lodged a complaint with the World Trade Organisation over China's protectionist film distribution practices. This March's decision in the US's favour prompted speculation over whether China would relax the strict quota system for the release of foreign films. And if it did, how would that affect local film-makers? It seems the Chinese film industry has responded by remembering a favourite teaching of ancient military philosopher Sun Tzu: attack is the best form of defence.

New Chinese Cinema

This month, *Legend of a Rabbit* will open in China, the first release from a 4.5bn yuan (#420m) animation facility developed by the Chinese state as—at least in part—a response to the success of the first *Kung Fu Panda* film. As a challenger to the big Hollywood studios, it will join Hengdian World Studios in Zhejiang province, which since the mid-1990s has steadily grown to become the world's largest outdoor film studio. *Crouching Tiger, Hidden Dragon* (2000), *Hero* (2002) and the American martial arts film *The Forbidden Kingdom* (2008) all made use of the complex's historical sets, which include a full-scale replica of the Forbidden City. To call it "Chinawood" would seem a tad reductive.

Why is the Chinese government investing so generously in cinema? As Hollywood's international reach proves, a healthy film industry extending a nation's cultural reach can be as useful to a nascent superpower as any number of nuclear warheads. Or, from a perspective less tinged with cold war nostalgia, China's economic prosperity affords it the opportunity to present its own image to the world, unmediated by Hollywood.

Not that it will be easy. "The western perceptions of China as an ageless rural country with a repressive 'red' regime remain a difficult obstacle for Chinese filmmakers—other than by designing these fantastic tales of martial arts set in ancient China," says Yingjin Zhang, author of *A Companion to Chinese Cinema*. Raymond Zhou, a film critic and columnist for the *China Daily* newspaper, agrees that using cinema to introduce the real China to the rest of the world may present some difficulties. "Traditional Chinese values are mainly non-confrontational and do not make good movies," he says. "It'll take a genius to tell a quintessential Chinese story on screen and be successful all over the world."

Could that genius be Zhang Yimou? A member of the first generation of directors to graduate from the reopened Beijing Film Academy following the Cultural Revolution, he is the most internationally successful director to emerge from mainland China, and along with Ang Lee, from Taiwan, among the most important Chinese-language directors working today. His 2002 film *Hero* opened at No 1 in the US box office, making it the second-highest grossing foreign-language film in US history (after Mel Gibson's *The Passion of the Christ*) while his 2004 followup *House of Flying Daggers* grossed a healthy $93m (#56m) worldwide.

Yet even a director of Zhang's standing has found that foreign interest dwindles when he strays too far from the martial arts (*wuxia*) formula. *A Woman, a Gun and a Noodle Shop*, Zhang's Gansu province-set remake of the Coen Brothers' 1984 film *Blood Simple*, made only a miniscule proportion of *Hero*'s $53m (#32m) box office and went straight to DVD in this country. Zhang chalks this up to cultural differences. "It's black humour and I think that has many local facets, like the language, the way they talk, the gestures and so on. So it's normal that people [in the US] don't get much of it. It didn't really bother me."

What matters for Chinese film-makers ... is not whether they will be able to reach foreign audiences, but whether they'll be able to satisfy their own.

Expectations are much higher for Zhang's latest film, *The Heroes of Nanking*, which is scheduled to wrap this week. A big-budget historical drama about the 1937 massacre of Chinese citizens by Japanese troops, it is no *wuxia* spectacular, but it does benefit from the presence of a western star in Christian Bale. Fresh from his Oscar win for *The Fighter*, Bale plays an American priest who helps hundreds of civilians escape death. *The Dark Knight* is yet to open in China (Warner Bros cited "cultural sensitivities"), but Bale has a following among young Chinese thanks to the country's vigorous trade in pirate DVDs, which have long been a key way for Chinese viewers to see foreign films.

An International Market

Zhang says *The Heroes of Nanking* was made with international audiences in mind. "First of all, the story is very international. It has a universal message about humanitarianism, about love and redemption, and also we have Christian Bale. And the other thing is almost half of it is in English." But the real strength of the film, says its Hollywood-based executive producer David Linde—who also worked on *Crouching Tiger, Hidden Dragon*—is that while its story is quintessentially Chinese, it has an appeal that transcends national borders. "A great signature director working with an incredibly inspiring actor? That in and of itself is thrilling. When do you get an opportunity where different cultures truly connect, in story, performance and direction? Really, very rarely."

It might seem unrealistic to expect US appetites for foreign film to broaden as fast as the Chinese appetite is growing, but Linde, who has worked with directors including Ang Lee, Pedro Almodóvar and Alfonso Cuarón, says there's hope. "There's clearly a real fascination with China. I don't know about England, but, as one small example, one of the things you're seeing a lot here is students increasingly studying Mandarin, instead of the more traditional French and Italian." And now that nervous jokes about a Mandarin-speaking future have become a mainstay of American political comedy, might curiosity about the new paymaster translate into box-office receipts? "I think that the opportunity for Chinese film-makers here is pretty significant."

What matters for Chinese film-makers, Zhang says, is not whether they will be able to reach foreign audiences, but whether they'll be able to satisfy their own. "The market is growing very fast and well-known directors don't necessarily develop at the same pace. We have an old Chinese saying: 'It takes 10 years to grow a tree, but 100 years to make a man.' Maybe this will break the limitation on internationally imported films, so we can have films from all over the world to fulfil the people's need."

That, of course, is where Hollywood steps in. When *The Heroes of Nanking* opens in the US, it will likely be accompanied by the rustle of both popcorn boxes and Hollywood screenwriters riffling through Chinese history books, on the hunt for suitable western characters. It can't be long before Reese Witherspoon is trading Mandarin quips with Tony Leung in her latest romantic comedy and James Cameron is directing Chow Yun Fat in a sci-fi blockbuster. When that happens, we'll know exactly which cuddly panda was responsible.

Organizations to Contact

The editors have compiled the following list of organizations concerned with the issues debated in this book. The descriptions are derived from materials provided by the organizations. All have publications or information available for interested readers. The list was compiled on the date of publication of the present volume; names, addresses, phone and fax numbers, and e-mail and Internet addresses may change. Be aware that many organizations take several weeks or longer to respond to inquiries, so allow as much time as possible.

American Enterprise Institute (AEI)

1150 17th St. NW, Washington, DC   20036
(202) 862-5800
e-mail: VRodman@aei.org
website: www.aei.org

The American Enterprise Institute (AEI) is a conservative public policy research organization dedicated to preserving and strengthening government, private enterprise, foreign policy, and national defense. Its Asian Studies Program focuses on the growing offensive capabilities of China's army, relations between Taiwan and mainland China, and economic and political reform in China. AEI's magazine, *American Enterprise*, covers developments in Asia, and the institute also publishes several books on China.

Asia Society

725 Park Ave., New York, NY   10021
(212) 288-6400 • fax: (212) 517-8315
e-mail: info@asiasociety.org
website: www.asiasociety.org

The Asia Society is an educational organization dedicated to fostering understanding of Asia and communication between Americans and the peoples of Asia and the Pacific. Reports and articles about China are available on its website.

China Daily

6/F, B3 Tower, Ziguang Building, No. 11 Huixin Dongjie
Chaoyang District, Beijing, PRC   100029
+86 (10) 84883300 • fax: +86 (10) 84883600
e-mail: yuanhui@chinadaily.com.cn
website: www.chinadaily.com.cn

China Daily is one of China's top nine news portals whose
mission is to connect China and the world. The website provides up-to-the-minute, in-depth news and information about
Chinese politics, economy, culture, entertainment, and lifestyle
to millions of online readers. It also covers international news
and provides in-depth analysis through columnists, opinions,
and editorials. Searches of the website lead the reader to a
wealth of articles and news reports about US-China trade and
relations.

Council on Foreign Relations

58 E. 68th St., New York, NY   10021
(212) 434-9400 • fax: (212) 434-9800
e-mail: communications@cfr.org
website: www.cfr.org

The Council on Foreign Relations researches the international
aspects of American economic and political policies. Its journal *Foreign Affairs*, published five times a year, provides analysis on global situations including those pertaining to China.

International Trade Administration (ITA)

US Department of Commerce, 1401 Constitution Ave. NW
Washington, DC   20230
(800) USA TRADE
website: http://trade.gov

Part of the US Department of Commerce, the International
Trade Administration's mission is to create prosperity by
strengthening the competitiveness of US industry, promoting
trade and investment, and ensuring fair trade and compliance
with trade laws and agreements. The ITA's website provides

information about US international trade policy, including trade statistics, press releases, speeches, and an online bookstore that provides access to various agency reports and studies. A search of the website produces numerous government publications on trading with China.

John L. Thornton China Center

Brookings Institution, 1775 Massachusetts Ave. NW
Washington, DC   20036
(202) 797-6000
e-mail: brookinfo@brook.edu
website: www.brookings.edu/china.aspx

The John L. Thornton China Center is a project of the Brookings Institution, a think tank that conducts research and education in the areas of foreign policy, economics, government, and the social sciences. The Center provides cutting-edge research, analysis, and dialogue focusing on China's emergence and the implications of this for the United States, China's neighbors, and the rest of the world. Its website features numerous publications on China, including *Managing the China Challenge: How to Achieve Corporate Success in the People's Republic* and *The Renminbi: The Political Economy of a Currency*.

United Nations Conference on Trade and Development (UNCTAD)

Palais des Nations, 8-14, Av. de la Paix, Geneva 10   1211
   Switzerland
+41 22 917 1234 • fax: +41 22 917 0057
e-mail: info@unctad.org
website: www.unctad.org

The United Nations Conference on Trade and Development (UNCTAD) was established by the United Nations (UN) to help integrate developing countries into the world economy. UNCTAD has addressed China's growing importance in the world economy in a number of informative analyses and publications, including *Key Issues in China's Economic Transformation, Trade and Development Report 2005* (which examines the underlying forces of China as a key player in the world economy) and *Trade and Development Report 2006* (which discusses the implications of different ways of correcting the existing global imbalances).

US Census Bureau, Foreign Trade Statistics

US Census Bureau, 4600 Silver Hill Rd.
Washington, DC 20233
(301) 763-4636
e-mail: pio@census.gov
website: www.census.gov/foreign-trade/index.html

Part of the US Census Bureau, the Foreign Trade Statistics division is a branch of the US government that compiles and disseminates statistical information about US trade. Among other publications, the division produces the *Guide to Foreign Trade Statistics*, which offers statistics on imports and exports on a country-by-country basis, including trade with China.

The US-China Business Council (USCBC)

1818 N St. NW, Suite 200, Washington, DC 20036
(202) 429-0340 • fax: (202) 775-2476
e-mail: info@uschina.org
website: www.uschina.org

The US-China Business Council (USCBC) is a private, non-profit organization of more than 250 American corporations that do business with China. Its mission is to expand the United States's commercial relationship with China to the benefit of the US economy. USCBC advocates a balanced approach to trade with China—one that expands opportunities while identifying and removing trade barriers. The website features a wide variety of statistical and policy reports, analyses, and other publications relevant to US-China trade relations.

US-China Economic and Security
Review Commission (USCC)

444 North Capitol St. NW, Suite 602, Washington, DC 20001
(202) 624-1407

e-mail: contact@uscc.gov
website: www.uscc.gov

The US-China Economic and Security Review Commission (USCC) was created in 2000 to monitor, investigate, and submit to Congress an annual report on the national security implications of the bilateral trade and economic relationship between the United States and the People's Republic of China, and to provide recommendations, where appropriate, to Congress for legislative and administrative action. The website offers a great deal of substantive information concerning the bilateral trade and economic relationship between the United States and China and outlines legislative and administrative action taken by Congress. Publications include annual reports to Congress, transcripts of congressional hearings and testimony, research papers, and press releases. Recent research, for example, includes *Backgrounder: China's 12th Five-Year Plan* and *Potential Health & Safety Impacts from Pharmaceuticals and Supplements Containing Chinese-Sourced Raw Ingredients.*

Bibliography

Books

Martin Jacques	*When China Rules the World: The End of the Western World and the Birth of a New Global Order*, rev. ed. New York: Penguin, 2012.
Henry Kissinger	*On China.* New York: Penguin, 2012.
Nicholas R. Lardy	*Sustaining China's Economic Growth After the Global Financial Crisis.* Washington, DC: Peterson Institute, 2012.
Ann Lee and Ian Bremmer	*What the U.S. Can Learn from China: An Open-Minded Guide to Treating Our Greatest Competitor as Our Greatest Teacher.* San Francisco: Berrett-Koehler, 2012.
Robyn Meredith	*The Elephant and the Dragon: The Rise of India and China and What It Means for All of Us.* New York: W.W. Norton, 2008.
John Milligan-Whyte and Dai Min	*US-China Relations in the Obama Administration: Facing Shared Challenges.* New York: New School Press Limited, 2011.
Imad Moosa	*US-China Trade Dispute: Facts, Figures and Myths.* Northampton, MA: Edward Elgar, 2012.

Russell Ong   *China's Strategic Competition with the United States.* New York: Routledge, 2011.

Shaun Rein   *The End of Cheap China: Economic and Cultural Trends That Will Disrupt the World.* Hoboken, NJ: Wiley, 2012.

Martin A. Smith   *Power in the Changing Global Order: The US, Russia and China.* Cambridge, UK: Polity, 2012.

John Bryan Starr   *Understanding China: A Guide to China's Economy, History, and Political Culture,* 3rd ed. New York: Hill and Wang, 2010.

Arvind   *Eclipse: Living in the Shadow of* Subramanian   *China's Economic Dominance.* Washington, DC: Institute of International Economics, 2011.

Edward Tse   *The China Stategy: Harnessing the Power of the World's Fastest-Growing Economy.* New York: Basic Books, 2010.

Carl Walter and   *Red Capitalism: The Fragile Financial* Fraser Howie   *Foundation of China's Extraordinary Rise,* rev. ed. Hoboken, NJ: Wiley, 2012.

Periodicals and Internet Sources

Asiamoney   "What Mitt Can Learn from China's Financial Diplomacy," September 2012.

Business Daily Update	"Erroneous Reports on the Yuan," October 17, 2012.
Business Daily Update	"Nike Hits China Roadblock, Shares Fall," September 28, 2012.
Business Daily Update	"Trade Official Calls on US, EU to Reject Protectionism," October 19, 2012.
John Cassidy	"Enter the Dragon," *New Yorker*, December 13, 2010.
Coral Davenport	"Obama-Romney Debate a Chance to Delve Into Global Energy," *National Journal*, October 19, 2012. www.nationaljournal.com.
Economist	"A Sigh of Relief: China and America," May 26, 2012.
Economist	"Turning from Green to Red: The Rise of the Yuan," October 20, 2012.
James Fallows	"China Takes Off," *Popular Science*, May 2012.
Financial Express	"Earnings in US Are Beginning to Feel a Pinch," September 18, 2012.
Fund Strategy	"Strategy: Take Care Against Emerging Risks," January 10, 2011.
Daniel Gross	"The Botox Economy," *Newsweek*, October 15, 2012.
Forrest Jones	"Chinese Inflation May Ease US Trade Deficit," *Newsmax*, January 31, 2011.

Nell Lukosavich   "Regional Report: China," *World Oil*, December 2011.

Jeff Moore   "Oil and Gas in the Capitals," *World Oil*, August 2011.

Treasury & Risk Breaking News   "Chinese Yuan Rises to 19-Year High," September 28, 2012.

WWD   "China-U.S. Trade Sees Tensions Rise," September 18, 2012. www.wwd.com.

Index